COURSE TECHNOLOGY
CENGAGE Learning·
Professional · Technical · Reference

Digital Painting Fundamentals with
Corel®
painter™11

Rhoda Grossman

COURSE TECHNOLOGY
CENGAGE Learning™

**Digital Painting Fundamentals
with Corel® Painter™ 11
Rhoda Grossman**

**Publisher and General Manager,
Course Technology PTR:**
Stacy L. Hiquet

Associate Director of Marketing:
Sarah Panella

Manager of Editorial Services:
Heather Talbot

Marketing Manager:
Jordan Casey

Acquisitions Editor:
Megan Belanger

Project Editor and Copy Editor:
Kim Benbow

Technical Reviewer:
Barbara Pollak

Editorial Services Coordinator:
Jen Blaney

Interior Layout:
Shawn Morningstar

Cover Designer:
Mike Tanamachi

CD-ROM Producer:
Brandon Penticuff

Indexer:
Larry Sweazy

Proofreader:
Gene Redding

For product information and technology assistance,
contact us at

**Cengage Learning Customer & Sales Support,
1-800-354-9706**

For permission to use material from this text or product,
submit all requests online at **cengage.com/permissions**

Further permissions questions can be emailed to
permissionrequest@cengage.com

Library of Congress Control Number: 2009924528

ISBN-13: 978-1-59863-893-6

ISBN-10: 1-59863-893-9

Course Technology, a part of Cengage Learning
20 Channel Center Street
Boston, MA 02210
USA

Cengage Learning is a leading provider of customized learning solutions with office locations around the globe, including Singapore, the United Kingdom, Australia, Mexico, Brazil, and Japan. Locate your local office at:
international.cengage.com/region

Cengage Learning products are represented in Canada by Nelson Education, Ltd.

For your lifelong learning solutions, visit **courseptr.com**
Visit our corporate website at **cengage.com**

Printed in the United States of America
1 2 3 4 5 6 7 11 10 09

In loving remembrance of my mother, Ida Levy.

Acknowledgments

I'm grateful to Stacy Hiquet and everybody at Cengage Learning for asking me to revise the first edition of my *Digital Painting Fundamentals* book for Painter 11. How fabulous to have a chance to take something pretty good and make it even better! Special thanks to my acquisitions editor Megan Belanger and my project editor Kim Benbow, both of whom were actually willing to work with me again. Thanks to Jordan Casey and her marketing team for the graphic design and layout and to Brandon Penticuff for designing the CD interface. For technical editing as well as a couple of nifty projects, I have my dear friend and colleague Barbara "Babs" Pollak to thank profusely. A tip of my sequined hat also goes to Carole Jelen, my agent at Waterside Productions.

Thanks, once again, to friends and family members who allowed me to use their likenesses for educational purposes. My deep appreciation (and admiration) also goes to Jerry Portnoy, master of the blues harmonica, for allowing me to photograph his collection of vintage microphones to use for an illustration project in Lesson 10. To Leo Arellano, DDS, I am grateful—not only for my dazzling smile but for the photos of my dental work used for the abstract painting project in Lesson 8.

I couldn't have done it without Rob MacDonald and his team at Corel Corporation who brought so many new features and improvements to Painter, the ultimate natural media software of and for digital artists. And finally, a very special thank-you goes to Wacom Technologies for setting the bar so high with regard to pressure-sensitive graphics tablets and for giving me so many freebies over the years.

About the Author

Rhoda Grossman is the author of numerous books and video tutorials on the creative uses of Corel Painter and Adobe Photoshop. Recent publications include the *Fun with Photoshop Elements* series and *Digital Painting Fundamentals with Corel Painter X*. She has taught basic drawing as well as computer graphics techniques at several schools in the San Francisco Bay Area and has earned a reputation for lively and humorous presentations. Rhoda became a "pixel-packin' mama" in 1990 and uses pixel-based software for commercial illustration and cartooning, as well as fine art projects. She has successfully transferred traditional figure-drawing skills to the computer and brings her MacBook Pro and Wacom tablet along to life drawing workshops where she specializes in quick gesture drawings. As "Rhoda Draws a Crowd," she creates digital caricature entertainment for trade shows and conventions. A member of the National Caricaturist Network (NCN), Rhoda is a pioneer in using digital media for live caricature at events, and she has won several awards from her professional colleagues. You can visit her website at www.digitalpainting.com.

Contents

Part II Beyond the Basics

9 Pixel-Based Animation 167

10 Illustration Projects............................189

A Fundamentals and Beyond 211

Introduction

This book will get you started with Corel Painter 11 as well as with other versions of the program. It provides step-by-step instruction for using the basic software and hardware that are the industry standards for pixel-based drawing and painting: Corel Painter and a Wacom graphics tablet. (If you're not sure what a graphics tablet is or what pixels are, please see this book's Appendix.) Exercises and projects will give you increasing control of tools and techniques. You will acquire and sharpen the skills needed for working in any medium, such as eye-hand coordination and drawing what you see. But there's more to digital art than just knowing how to make a series of marks on an electronic canvas—you will also be introduced to traditional art concepts, such as composition, line quality, contrast, and focal point.

With digital art, there's no need for stretching canvases or preparing a surface to accept pigment. You won't need to replenish dried-up tubes of paint or replace broken chalks and worn-out brushes. Your clothes won't get spattered with ink, you never need to inhale toxic fumes, and your hands will stay clean. (For artists who would actually miss the messiness of a traditional studio, Wacom might be working on making a pressure-sensitive leaky pen that smells like turpentine!) You can save every version of a painting as it develops. Your digital paper won't wrinkle, your colors won't fade, and with 32 levels of Undo, there's no such thing as a mistake. As for storage space, thousands of drawings and paintings can fit into a few cubic inches of a hard drive or on CDs.

A Little History

Unleashed in the early 1990s, Painter brought forth a new era for pixel-based digital graphics. Painter was the first *natural media emulation* program, created for artists by artists! With this software, along with the newly developed pressure-sensitive graphics tablets to replace the mouse, artists could begin to work comfortably at the computer. Painter has matured over the years, surviving the transfer from its parent company, Fractal Design, to Corel Corporation, and remains unrivalled for its capacity to imitate virtually any natural medium. (It also has a considerable number of bells and whistles for creating effects that go way beyond what can be produced "naturally.")

When Painter was released, I was in the right place at the right time (for a change), creating digital caricatures as a booth attraction for computer graphics trade shows. I painted with Photoshop then, but when I saw what Painter could do, I knew what my future looked like (for a change). I still rely on Photoshop for image manipulation, but Photoshop's Brush tool is anemic compared to Painter's robust array of brush styles and controls. Incidentally, these two apps have become more and more compatible with each other over the years. You can create an image in either program, then open it in the other for additional work, using the best features of each. Taken together, Photoshop and Painter are the Dream Team for pixel-pushers.

I've written books and tutorials on both Photoshop and Painter for over a decade, and I've taught both digital and traditional art skills in the classroom during most of that time. I began developing a curriculum for teaching traditional art fundamentals in a digital environment about seven years ago. *Digital Painting Fundamentals with Corel Painter 11* represents the culmination of that effort. The first edition, which focused on Painter X, was greeted with considerable enthusiasm by users who enjoyed my friendly and humorous teaching style. Amazon.com customer reviews of the first edition included such comments as "totally unintimidating," "she gets right to the point," and "from page one I was hooked." Not all of those glowing reviews were written by my friends and family. Anyhow, this incarnation of *Digital Painting Fundamentals* is even better.

Who Needs This Book?

If you are in one or more of the following groups, this book is for you.

- Traditional fine artists and illustrators getting ready to "go digital," or at least willing to give it a try

- Novice or intermediate users of Corel Painter and Wacom tablets with little or no art background

- Photoshop users who want to enhance their creativity with the "other" pixel-based program

- Health-conscious people who are literally sick and tired of using toxic art supplies

- Folks who bought the previous edition of this book and want to see how many of the typos got fixed

Others who would be well advised to choose this book as their introduction to Corel Painter are impatient users who don't want to sit through an interminable explanation of every nook and cranny of the program before they're allowed to get their feet wet. In this book, you're invited to jump in and splash around almost immediately. If you enjoy the instant gratification of your creative impulses, Painter is just the ticket! Using a Wacom tablet with Painter is so intuitive, young children can get the hang of it in a few minutes. I gave a hands-on workshop at Zeum, a children's multimedia and technology museum in San Francisco, and these kids could create awesome stuff—if their parents got out of the way.

When traditional artists get a glimpse of the enormous capabilities of Corel Painter, they can usually overcome any fear of technology that might stand in their way—it happened to me 18 years ago. I was a technophobic artist/illustrator who became suddenly intrigued with digital art in middle-age and managed to create a new career path with my "beginner's mind" and the courage to explore unknown territory. I am now an official tour guide to that territory. But I'm still not really a "techie," and that makes me an ideal trainer for people who need a little hand holding to break into digital art. This book will help traditional artists transfer their skills to the computer. It will also show folks who think they have no "talent" that they can learn the basics. . .then it's just practice, practice, practice. I am convinced that if you are computer literate, you can learn to draw and paint digitally if you can set aside fears, insecurities, and negative judgments about your readiness and self-worth. (Oops, is my background in psychology showing?)

No prior experience with Painter or other graphics applications is required. Oh, yes—you'll need a Wacom tablet, unless you really prefer drawing with a bar of soap or a hockey puck.

What You Will Learn

Although the word "drawing" doesn't appear in the title of this book, drawing is an essential foundation for painting. Drawing ability, like many skills, is a combination of natural aptitude and training. We don't expect a pianist to simply sit down and play a concerto without years of study and practice, including scales and fingering exercises. Lesson 1, "Welcome to Painter," provides exercises and the graphic equivalent of musical scales to practice eye-hand coordination, control, and technique. Use these exercises for a few minutes before each session to warm up and loosen up before you begin to work. You might never play the piano, but you'll be able to draw one.

Lesson 2, "Basic Drawing," introduces basic drawing techniques that you will continue to use throughout the book. If you already have skill using traditional art materials, you'll find it easier to master digital media. If you don't have traditional drawing or painting expertise, you can begin to develop it here. Drawing and painting techniques can be learned and improved by anyone at any age.

Famous drawing teachers like Betty Edwards (*Drawing on the Right Side of the Brain*, originally published by Tarcher, 1979) agree that the ability to draw is based in large part on the ability to see accurately. In these lessons, you will be encouraged to develop your ability to look critically at your subject, whether it's a still life or a nude model, and observe the shapes, lines, textures, tones, and proportions that are essential to making a successful drawing. With practice, you will be able to improve your ability to see your subject and interpret what you see.

The projects presented in these lessons begin with simple assignments and gradually become more challenging. They cover a wide range of subjects and techniques, including the following:

- Tracing a photo

- Sketching a still life

- Painting a landscape

- Creating a portrait

- Drawing the human figure

- Cloning a photo in different styles

- Abstract painting

- Illustration and graphic techniques

- Experimental animation

- Mixed media self-portrait

Personal fulfillment and More

Sadly, public schools don't offer much to nurture creativity. Art (and, to a lesser extent, music) is neglected and discounted as an esoteric pursuit reserved for the rare person who is "talented" from birth. Most people go through life thinking they have no such talent, while the truth is that they simply haven't learned some basic skills and concepts that can be mastered with practice. Creative expression is not only important for personal fulfillment, but it's also a valuable element in a healthy society.

This book is not an exhaustive encyclopedia of Painter, so keep your user guide handy. In order to keep the focus on drawing and painting, I didn't even try to present every aspect of the program. Our main course is exploring the natural media brushes, with special effects and image manipulation as side dishes. You'll have the opportunity to peek under the hood at Painter's brush engine when you're ready, and I'll show you how the controls work so you can customize your brushes. By the time you finish all the projects in all the lessons, from soup to nuts, you will have digested most Painter techniques and had a nibble of many others. You'll probably find some brushes and tools more to your taste than others. And if you're still hungry for more instruction, there is a menu of resources in the Appendix.

How to Use This Book

Working in order, Lessons 1, 2, and 3, "Working with Layers," will give you enough of the fundamentals to get you off and running. After that you can feel free to jump around and do what looks interesting at any given moment. Within a lesson, it's a good idea to start with the first project and work sequentially, but even that isn't absolutely required.

Each project is liberally illustrated with images at various stages to keep you on track. Screen captures of dialog boxes, menus, and palettes will help you navigate the program and choose options. These screenshots were all made on a Mac, but the difference between them and the Windows version is merely cosmetic. In any case, I'll give keyboard commands for both Mac and PC. For example, Command/Ctrl means use the Command key if you're on a Mac, the Ctrl key if you use Windows. Including the keystroke equivalent every time I mention a command will be awkward, so I added a list of the most popular keyboard shortcuts to the Appendix.

This book focuses on Corel Painter 11, but users of versions 8 through X will be in a familiar environment and can work all the projects, even if some advanced brushes or features are not available. Photoshop users will find that a great many Painter tools, palettes, and commands are the same or similar to what they are accustomed to. In a few special cases, I couldn't help mentioning how each program handles a task differently, but you won't find extensive comparisons between Painter and Photoshop here. That's beyond the scope of this book.

The Appendix has some suggestions for customizing Painter preferences to suit the way you like to work. Use the default settings for a while if you're not sure about these choices. Some basic terms and definitions can be found there, along with other handy bits of information. There are resources for images, fonts, and printing, and even a little free legal advice. I also list other books and publications to help you develop as a digital artist, so take a look back there once in a while.

What's on the CD?

Here's where you'll find the source images needed for all projects, organized by lesson number and by subject categories. There are photos of people, places, and things, mostly shot by me (so I could deduct my camera as a business expense). Some of the images were donated by family and friends. In addition to the specific images I use in each lesson, many more photos are provided for you to choose from or to use in your own projects. You are encouraged to use your own source images for some projects, especially for the self-portrait.

Corel Painter provides ways to organize your favorite tools and art materials. The Palettes and Libs folder on the CD contains custom palettes and libraries to accompany specific projects, making it easier for you to jump right into a lesson without having to rummage around searching for the recommended brushes, colors, and other items. You'll learn how easy it is to create your own custom palettes and libraries, too.

The Rhoda Portfolio folder has samples of my digital art created in successive versions of Painter, spanning about 17 years. These show my use of several styles, showcasing the range and versatility of Painter. You'll see some illustration assignments as well as personal projects, portraits, abstract painting, cartooning, and experimental caricature created live at trade shows and other events.

But enough about me. I'll see you in Lesson 1.

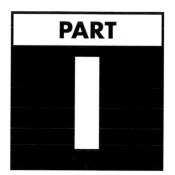

PART
I

The Basics

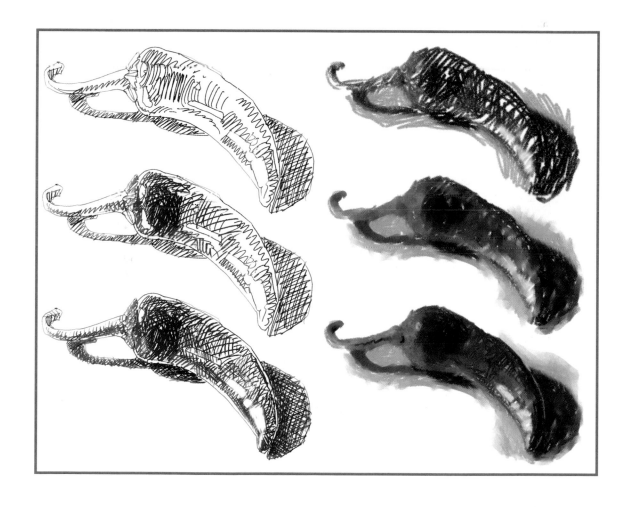

1 Welcome to Painter

If you read the Introduction, then you know this book addresses the most recent version of Painter, Corel's powerful software for natural media sketching and painting. You are also aware that a pressure-sensitive tablet is necessary for working effectively with Painter—any Wacom tablet will be fine. If you didn't read the Introduction, I admire your eagerness to get right to the main course. But trust me, there are some tasty appetizers in those opening remarks. Lesson 1 will still be nice and warm when you get back.

I made these scribbles with just a few of the brush variants available in most versions of Painter. In just a few minutes, you'll be able to create digital scribbles as good as this! So, launch your Painter program and let's get started.

You'll need a blank canvas to work on. When the Welcome screen comes up, choose **Create New Document**. If you don't get a Welcome screen, just choose **File > New (Cmd/Ctrl+N)**. The New dialog box, shown in Figure 1.1, lets you enter height, width, and resolution for the image. We'll use 72 ppi most of the time, so you'll be able to see the whole image on screen without scrolling and you can work faster. (Pixels and resolution are explained in the Appendix.)

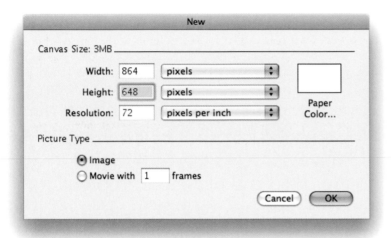

Figure 1.1

Choose size and resolution for your new canvas.

Hide and Seek

If you don't see a palette you need, scroll down the list in the Window menu until you find it. This should toggle it on. Palettes that are open have a check mark next to their name in the list. Earlier versions of Painter use "Show" and "Hide" to indicate a palette's visibility.

Figure 1.2

The Brush tool lets
you make your mark.

Getting Acquainted

In addition to your canvas, the Painter workspace consists of several palettes offering brushes and other art supplies as well as special features and commands. All palettes are listed in the **Window** menu and can be organized any way you like. (I'll talk about customizing palettes later.) You'll see the vertical Toolbox on the left side of your screen. Make sure the **Brush tool** is selected, as shown in Figure 1.2. If all you want to do is draw and paint, you can ignore all the other choices in the Toolbox for quite a while.

Working with Painter, you will have only one actual tool in your hand—the Wacom pen. Hold it as shown in Figure 1.3. Avoid touching the lever on the side of the pen's barrel. (It has click functions that won't be useful while you're drawing.) This model is the Intuos 3 with a 6x8-inch active area—my preferred size. Pressure sensitivity enables you to control the width and/or opacity of your stroke by varying how hard you press the tip of the pen to the tablet as you work.

Figure 1.3

Wacom tablet and pen.

The marks you make with your Wacom pen can imitate virtually any traditional art materials. Traditional (analog) tools for drawing and painting include a wide variety of pencils, pens, brushes, and sticks. They differ greatly in the kinds of marks they can make and the type of material they can mark: paper, canvas, or boards, with various surface textures. You'll choose your digital "brush" with the **Brush Selector Bar** in the upper-right corner of the Painter workspace. It has two sections: one for the category and the other for the specific variant within that category. Figure 1.4 shows that the **Design Marker** (20 pixels size) in the **Felt Pens** category is the current "brush." Each category has a distinctive icon, and the shape of the variant's tip is also shown. That black rectangle means the Design Marker has a chisel shape.

When Is a Brush Not a Brush?

When it's a pencil, or a pen, or a piece of chalk! Painter uses the term *brush* in a generic way to refer to everything used for drawing and painting on your digital canvas.

Figure 1.4

The Brush Selector Bar shows the current category and variant.

Let's Doodle

Click on the **Brush Category** section to see the long list of options. Figure 1.5 shows most of them. Look over the list to get a feel for how many choices you have, but don't let that scare you! Move your cursor to **Pens** and click to choose that group. Now click on the **Brush Variant** section and choose **Thick n Thin Pen 5,** as in Figure 1.6. Make some strokes and squiggles on your canvas, changing the pressure and speed of your pen.

Figure 1.5

There are 37 brush categories in Painter 11.

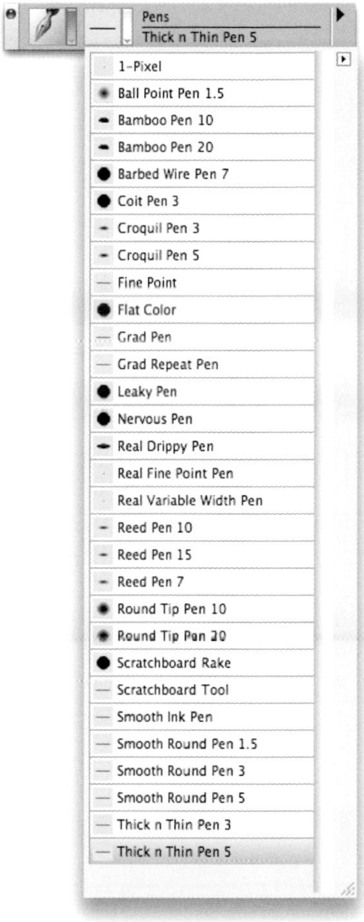

Figure 1.6

Choose Thick n Thin Pen 5 from
the Pens category.

Figure 1.7 has scribbles made with the **Thick n Thin Pen 5.**
We expect pens to make smooth lines that might have thick-
and-thin variation based on the tip shape or pressure applied.
This variant also shows opacity changes as a function of
pressure, imitating traditional nib pens that are dipped into
an inkwell.

Figure 1.7
Thick n Thin Pen 5 practice.

I Love the Pressure!

Did your pen strokes respond to pressure variations? Even more important, did the lines appear where you wanted them? Use the "Test Your Tablet" note to confirm that your Wacom tablet is functioning properly.

If the pen strokes required more pressure than you're comfortable with, or (on the other hand) if the pen seems too sensitive to pressure changes, you can customize the tablet's sensitivity within Painter. Click on **Corel Painter** in the menu strip and find **Preferences > Brush Tracking**. Make a stroke in the rectangle shown in Figure 1.8, and Painter will automatically adjust to your touch! It's a good idea to do this whenever you change the way you work. Now try some more pen strokes on the canvas, and see if that helped. Painter X and 11 actually remember your touch between sessions.

Test Your Tablet

Make sure the tablet is mapped to your computer screen by doing the "two-point test." Touch the point of your pen to any corner of the active area of the tablet and notice that your cursor shows up at the corresponding corner of your screen. That was one point. (If that didn't work, you're in trouble—see the Wacom tablet section in the Appendix.) Now lift the pen away from the tablet (don't drag it!) and touch it to the opposite/diagonal corner. If the cursor shows up in the new position, you're good to go. If not, see the Appendix.

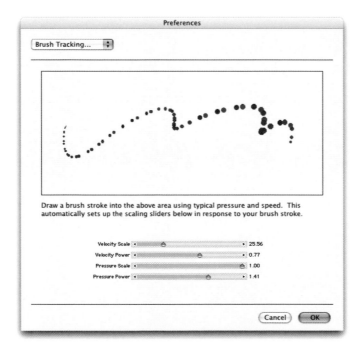

Figure 1.8

Customize your pen pressure and speed.

Meanwhile, Back at the Palettes

Just below the Brush Selector Bar is a set of palettes for choosing colors. The default Color Picker shown in Figure 1.9 has a Hue (H) ring with a movable indicator (the transparent rectangle) showing your color's position on the spectrum. The triangle inside the Hue ring has another indicator (the hollow circle with crosshairs) for Saturation (S) and Value (V), also called Brightness or Luminosity. To choose a new color, drag either of those indicators to a new position. Or you can drag the R, G, and B sliders to control the red, green, and blue components of a color. Type the numerical values for R, G, and B to match a specific color. The popup menu on the Colors palette lets you switch to HSV display. The little swatches at the lower-left show the current main color is a rich magenta. See the Appendix for more info on color.

You might prefer to pick colors from an array of swatches called Color Sets. Figure 1.10 shows this palette open along with a menu of choices for switching to a different Color Set or creating your own. All Painter palettes are managed by clicking on those little triangles, circles, and X-boxes.

Figure 1.9
Pick a color, any color.

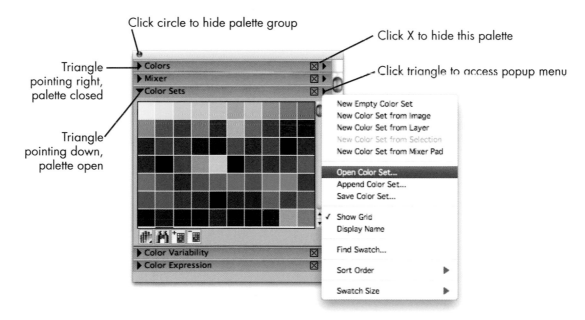

Figure 1.10
Switch to swatches.

Pencils and Markers and Chalk—Oh My!

Dry media, such as pencils and chalk, respond to pressure changes with variation in opacity. Figure 1.11 has marks made with **Pencils > Grainy Pencil 5** and **Chalk > Square Chalk 35**. In real life, overlapping pencil or crayon strokes build up, getting darker and denser. By contrast, chalk and pastels are opaque, so light colors can cover darker strokes. Notice that pink chalk strokes are able to cover up the darker brown underneath, but the same pink applied with a pencil gets even darker. Painter uses the terms *cover* and *buildup* to describe these two basic methods for determining the behavior of a brush variant. Do felt markers use the cover or buildup method? If you're not sure, or even if you are, test one of the variants in the **Felt Pens** category. Make overlapping strokes with any light color and see what happens.

Figure 1.11
Pencils and chalk.

We expect pencils and chalk to reveal the surface texture of the paper we are using, and digital dry media behave as expected. Painter uses the term *grainy* for this brush behavior. I used three different paper textures—Basic Paper, Artists' Canvas, and Pebbleboard. The results are especially dramatic with the wide chalk marks on the right. Lighter pressure reveals more of the paper surface because heavy strokes tend to fill in the depressions. **Basic Paper** has a subtle grain and is the default texture. Choose a different type of surface from the **Paper Selector** near the bottom of the **Toolbox**, or open the **Papers** palette by choosing **Window > Library Palettes > Show Papers**. Figure 1.12 has the current paper library open to show thumbnail swatches.

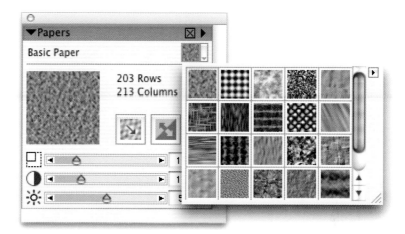

Figure 1.12
Pick your paper.

When Is Paper Not Paper?

When it's canvas or pavement or wood! Of course, you can draw and paint on a variety of surfaces that aren't paper. Painter uses the term generically, referring to any surface texture. The word "grainy" describes brush variants that can reveal texture, but "grainy" might not always be part of the variant's name.

Real Brushes (Almost)

Traditional brushes can have a variety of shapes and are composed of numerous bristles that can range in length, thickness, and stiffness. The kind of mark made by a brush depends on a large number of factors: quality and number of bristles, viscosity and amount of paint loaded, and pressure and direction of the artist's stroke. There are several categories devoted to bristle-type brushes. They include Oils, Artists' Oils, Acrylic, Impasto (Italian for *thick paint*), and the intriguingly named RealBristle Brushes. I made the orange and pink strokes in Figure 1.13 with **Oils > Smeary Flat.** Choose that variant, and notice that the shape of the tip is a compressed vertical oval, like a plump grain of rice. I made half a dozen marks using only the tip of the brush by pressing down hard with my Wacom pen and jiggling it just a little. When you paint horizontally, the **Smeary Flat Oils** stroke looks light and airy, but it is dense and smooth when you make vertical marks. Go ahead and give this brush a test drive. Switch to another color to see how overlapping strokes behave. The color of your stroke is influenced by the color underneath. My orange marks are pale when I begin on the white background, but darker when I start dragging on a red area.

Figure 1.13
Different strokes.

Now choose **Artists' Oils > Oily Bristle.** The trailing off of those long blue and violet squiggles is not the result of reduced pen pressure—this brush actually runs out of paint! Compare these two brushes. Oily Bristle has more translucency than Smeary Flat. Both of them have a "smeary" quality, so underlying color mixes with a new stroke.

Okay, let's get really messy now. Choose **Real Oils Smeary** from the **RealBristle Brushes** category. Nothing much happens if you paint on a plain white section of the canvas. But when you scribble over several existing strokes of different colors, things get exciting in a hurry.

So Many Choices!

Every new version of Painter has more brush categories and variants than the previous version. There are hundreds to choose from. Just exploring a fraction of them and keeping track of the ones you like can be a challenge. Fortunately, every new version of the program also provides increasingly better ways to organize brushes and customize the workspace. Yes, you even have more choices for how to choose!

Keeping Track

Painter lets you find recently used and favorite brushes without having to search through all those lists in the Brush Selector Bar. Open the **Tracker** palette from the **Window** menu to see a list of the brush variants you have used so far. To return to a previous brush, simply click on its name in the Tracker. Figure 1.14 shows my Tracker during a recent work session.

Click on the little black triangle on the right of the Tracker title bar to access some handy options. Brushes you want to use over and over can be locked, while others can be cleared from the list to keep it slim and trim. The Tracker palette remembers your most recently used brushes even between work sessions.

Figure 1.14

Automatic brush tracking.

Custom Palettes

After you've been working with Painter for a while, maybe tomorrow, you'll probably know what your favorite brushes, papers, and other art materials are. All of these can be combined in a compact little palette that is saved automatically. Custom palettes are easy to make. Choose the brush variant you want, and drag its icon away from the Brush Selector Bar. A new custom palette is created containing that brush. Add more brushes by simply dragging in more items. Hold the Shift key down to remove or reposition items. Figure 1.15 shows how I created a custom palette with most of my scribble brushes. I dragged a few of my favorite paper textures in, too.

Drag either the category icon or the variant icon to your canvas.

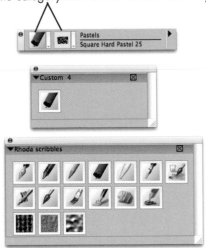

Figure 1.15

Make a custom palette.

Figure 1.16

Get organized.

Have It Your Way

Custom palettes are very versatile. You might want to have a different custom palette for sketching, painting, working with photos, or for a specific project. No problem. Manage them with the **Custom Palette Organizer** by choosing **Window > Custom Palette > Organizer**. Figure 1.16 shows my Scribbles palette highlighted and ready to be saved to a folder with other custom palettes, using the **Export** command. It's available on the CD that accompanies this book. Load it now, using the **Import** command.

Back to the Drawing Board

Continue exploring more brushes, using the Scribbles custom palette for help in making your selections. Here's a list of the brushes I used, in no special order, showing both the category and variant. (I'm leaving out the pixel sizes.) As you sample each of them, see if you can match them to the strokes and squiggles I made. You don't need to imitate my scribbles, just identify them.

- Pens > Thick n Thin Pen
- Pencils > Grainy Pencil
- Crayons > Dull Crayon
- Pastels > Square Hard Pastel
- Airbrushes > Finer Spray
- Calligraphy > Dry Ink
- Artists > Van Gogh, Impressionist, Seurat, Sargent Brush
- Blenders > Pointed Stump
- Real Bristle Brushes > Real Oils Smeary
- Digital Watercolor > New Simple Water
- Impasto > Gloopy
- Artists' Oils > Oily Bristle
- Oils > Smeary Flat

Just Sampling

Your first assignment is to create a "sampler" using each of the brushes in the Scribbles palette at least once. To help make something more pleasing to the eye, restrict yourself to one color. A monochromatic piece tends to have visual harmony even with lots of variety in brush strokes, texture, and detail. I chose a warm golden yellow to begin the painting in Figure 1.17. You may change the saturation and brightness of the main color by clicking in the triangle of the Color Picker, but stick with the same position on the Hue ring.

Figure 1.17
Mano a mono.

I love the brushes in the Artists category, designed to imitate some famous artists and styles. I use four of them in my golden sampler and near the bottom of the scribbles page. The Van Gogh brush is composed of several parallel strokes with some slight variation in hue and value (brightness). Each stroke creates a random combination of those colors, so I recommend applying short overlapping strokes, as in Figure 1.18. I increased the default size of the brush. The Impressionist brush is composed of a narrow spray of tear-drop shaped dabs, which follow the direction of your stroke. The Seurat brush is named after the French painter who invented the technique of pointillism, where tiny dots of color combine optically for the viewer. This brush sprays overlapping dots of variable color. The Sargent brush, a tribute to the portrait painter John Singer Sargent, has no built-in color variation but does have a smeary quality that contributes to its creamy, luscious look.

Here's a trick most Photoshop users know for changing the size of your current brush on the fly with your keyboard—use the bracket keys. The left bracket ([) makes the brush a bit smaller, and the right bracket (]) makes it larger.

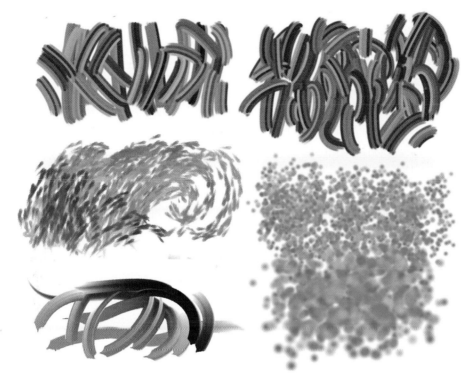

Figure 1.18

Famous artists.

Proceed at Your Own Risk!

You can explore other brush categories now, or any time, but be warned—some of them are pretty wacky! For example, **Pattern Pens** don't apply the current color but paint with the current pattern (you'll find that library right under Papers at the bottom of the Toolbox). **Watercolor** brushes require a special layer, created automatically when you use one of them. Then you have to switch back to the Canvas layer to use non-Watercolor brushes. But **Digital Watercolor** variants can be applied directly to the canvas, needing no special layer. **Liquid Ink** is in a class (and layer) by itself. Well, you get the idea.

Control Yourself

Here are some exercises I recommend for developing skill with the Wacom tablet. Use them as a warm-up before you begin a work session, and to check whether you need to reset the Brush Tracker (not to be confused with the Tracker palette) for your pressure and speed. Do the exercises in the order given. If you save them, you can observe your progress from one session to another.

Crosshatched Scribbles

Start with a new white canvas at least 6 inches square at 72 ppi. Choose **Pen > Ball Point Pen 1.5** and use black as the primary color. Refer to Figure 1.19 as you work. For your first stroke make a rapid saw tooth vertical scribble that fills most of the canvas. You'll have better control if you support the side of your hand on the tablet and slide up and down. (Notice that the Ball Point Pen doesn't respond much to pressure changes, just like its real-world counterpart.) This first stroke should remind you of Bart Simpson needing a haircut. Your second stroke goes over the first, but it is horizontal. Then make each of the diagonal strokes on top of that. At this point your canvas should look like the lower left corner of Figure 1.19.

Figure 1.19
Scribble and smear practice.

Now switch to a brush that smears without adding color: **Blenders > Grainy Water**. Working on top of the same crosshatch scribble, repeat those four strokes again—vertical, horizontal, and two diagonals—for the result in the lower right of Figure 1.19. That loosened you up, didn't it?

Practice Your Scales

Drawing is a lot like playing a musical instrument—ya gotta practice, practice. With that comparison in mind, let's do some scales! Begin with a new canvas or simply eliminate your previous scribbles quickly with **Select > All (Cmd/Ctrl+A)** followed by pressing the **Delete (Backspace)** key.

This exercise will help you develop an accurate placement of strokes. Let's use a Pencil variant this time and a bright color. I used a **Greasy Pencil** to make the rows of scales in Figure 1.20. Make a series of vertical scalloped curves, starting either at the top or the bottom. Working horizontally is okay, too. Switch direction (color, too) just for variety. If it's easier for you to work from left to right, try going the other way to challenge yourself. Fill up the canvas with scales of different sizes. I love that Greasy Pencil! With a little more practice, I bet I could work up a really good chain-link fence effect.

Figure 1.20

Nonmusical scales.

Pressure Control

Dry Ink is one of my favorite brush variants. One of the things I love about it is the extreme variation in stroke thickness, as a function of pressure. You'll find it, for some strange reason, in the **Calligraphy** category. Clear your canvas once again, or start a new one. Make a long horizontal stroke that begins with light pen pressure and gradually increase pressure to the maximum as you end the stroke. My first practice stroke in Figure 1.21 shows an abrupt change in thickness, looking more like a corn dog than a tadpole. It might take several tries to get the right touch for a smooth transition. Alternate right-to-left strokes with left-to-right and try vertical strokes as well. Can you make a stroke that begins thin, swells to full width and then tapers off?

Can You Handle the Pressure?

Making smooth transitions in line width is more challenging if you're working with a smaller tablet, or models with fewer pressure levels (the Bamboo Fun series). If that's the case, it's especially important to tweak sensitivity of the tablet with **Preferences > Brush Tracking**.

Figure 1.21
Dry ink under pressure.

Make a Warm-Up Palette

Recall the custom palettes feature we explored earlier in this lesson? Refer to Figure 1.15 as a guide to making one for your warm-up brushes. The brushes I used for the exercises were as follows:

- Pens > Ball Point 1.5

- Blenders > Grainy Water

- Pencils > Greasy Pencil (any size)

- Calligraphy > Dry Ink

Is **Dry Ink** still your current brush? Drag its icon away from the **Brush Selector** to start a custom palette, then add each of the other three variants. If they aren't in the order you want, reposition an item by holding down the Shift key as you drag it. The Shift key allows you to remove items, also. Give your new custom palette a descriptive name with the **Custom Palette Organizer**. Figure 1.22 shows the New Palette field for typing in any name you like.

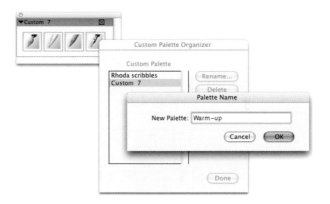

Figure 1.22
Rename the palette.

What's Next?

You're off to a good start. You have a basic understanding of how to choose and organize Painter brushes and how to show your Wacom tablet who's boss. You've already created an abstract monochromatic work of art. I hope you saved it! In the following lessons, you'll practice skills and learn concepts for improving your mastery of drawing and painting. I promise to take you way beyond scribbling!

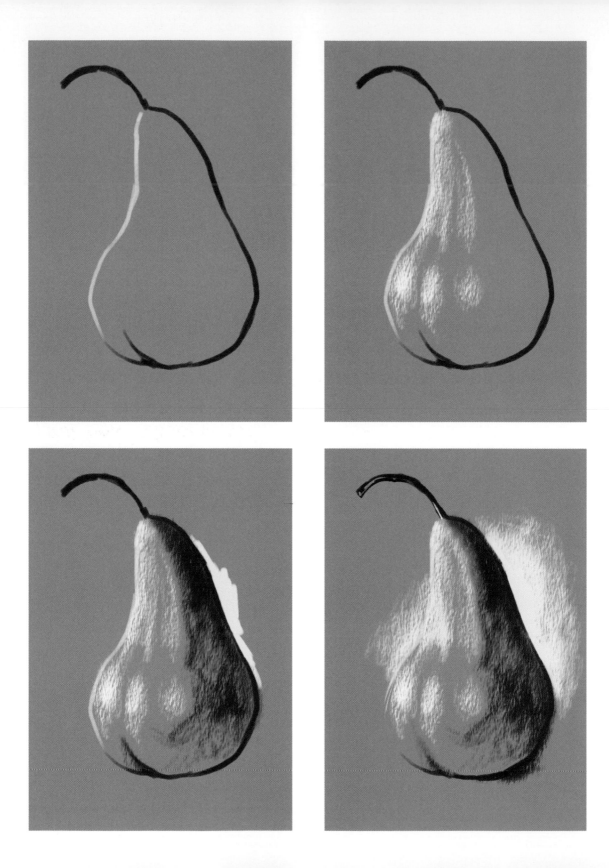

2 Basic Drawing

We'll start with a simple subject and practice drawing it using several methods. Painter offers beginners some "training wheels." Use them as long as you want. When you're feeling less wobbly, simply take them off and draw freely.

The Pear

Open **Pear.jpg** from the source images folder on the CD that accompanies this book. It's a good example of a simple still life subject (see Figure 2.1). It looks good enough to eat, and draw (not necessarily in that order). There are other delicious images in the Produce section of the folder. All are ripe for the picking—and painting.

Size Matters

You may want to change the size of the pear image to fit your screen. That's easy. **Canvas > Resize** brings up the dialog box shown in Figure 2.2. Before you enter the new height or width, be sure to uncheck the **Constrain File Size** box. If you don't, the change in dimensions will be compensated with a change in resolution, and the image will be exactly the same size on screen!

Figure 2.1
A classic subject.

Figure 2.2
Don't constrain file size.

Clone and Trace

Take a good look at the pear. Ignore the bruises and scratches, but focus on the edges of the shape. It is made up of a series of curves. The easiest way to make a simple outline of this shape is to trace it, and the easiest way to set up Painter's **Tracing Paper** function is **File > Quick Clone.** Painter automatically creates an exact copy of the image, names it "Clone of pear.jpg" and deletes the image to give you a blank canvas. You will see the original pear at 50% opacity, however, because the tracing paper feature is on. Keep the original (**Clone Source**) open while you work on the clone. Figure 2.3 points out the icon that toggles tracing paper on or off (keyboard shortcut is **Cmd/Ctrl+T**), which you'll need to do as your sketch develops.

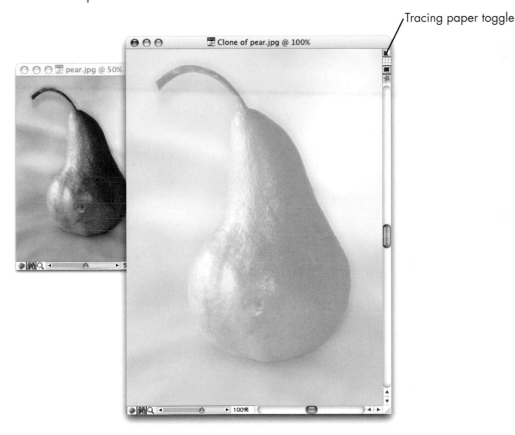

Tracing paper toggle

Figure 2.3

Tracing paper at 50% opacity.

Opacity Capacity

Painter X introduced changeable opacity for tracing paper. Just hold down the tracing paper icon to choose thicker or thinner paper. Percentage indicates hiding power, so the higher the value, the more opaque the tracing paper and the less you can see the original image. This is a handy feature for accommodating different stages in your drawing or different kinds of source images.

So, you just need to pick a brush variant and a color, and you're ready to trace. I chose a rich brown, sampled from the shadow side of the pear source image. You don't have to actually switch to the **Dropper** tool to pick a color from an open image—just hold down the **Opt/Alt** key and your brush cursor becomes a dropper. After you click on the color you want, release the modifier key and it's a **Brush** tool again.

Use a **Crayon**, **Pencil,** or **Colored Pencil** variant for lines that show paper grain. My simple sketch in Figure 2.4 was done with **Sharp Colored Pencil 7**. I started with the stem, using heavy pressure and several strokes to add thickness. It took three curved strokes to draw the right side of the fruit, then I overlapped a couple of strokes to emphasize weight at the bottom of the shape. A hint of the pear's "cleavage" was made with very light pressure. Don't forget to turn off tracing paper to see your drawing!

Dude! Where's My Clone Source?

If you accidentally close the source image while you're working, or if the relationship between the source and the clone gets "broken" for any reason, reconnecting them is easy. Open the source image again and use **File > Clone Source** to designate it as the one you want for reference.

Figure 2.4
Pear-shaped.

Tonal Drawing

The outline drawing looks flat. Examine the pear photo again, and this time notice the areas of light and shadow. We'll do another drawing that emphasizes these light and dark shapes, so we can create the illusion of depth. A traditional way to render light and dark effectively involves working on medium gray or tinted paper. Paper color does a lot of the work, and all you have to do is add the lightest and darkest parts.

Save your outline drawing, if you wish, and make the original pear photo the target image. Use the **Quick Clone** command again for a fresh canvas. Sample a medium to light orange color from the left side of the fruit, but not the brightest part. Choose **Set Paper Color** from the **Canvas** menu. Nothing happens yet, but when you **Select > All** (**Cmd/Ctrl +A**) and delete, your new color will fill the blank canvas. (Painter defines Paper Color as the color revealed by an Eraser. So, you just erased the whole image.)

This time I'm using a Conte stick for the dark brown outline, but I switched to white for the left edge, indicating the light source. Real French Conte sticks are firmer and creamier than chalk or charcoal, and Painter creates the illusion digitally quite well. Figure 2.5 was done with **Tapered Conte 8.** That white line implies volume, like an embossed shape raised a bit from the paper surface.

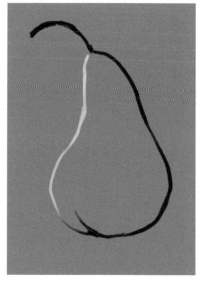

Figure 2.5
A hint of depth.

Serial Save

A great new feature introduced in version 11 is **Iterative Save** in the **File** menu. When you want to save stages in the development of an image, this command automatically numbers each version in order. Use the keyboard shortcut **Option+Cmd+S/Alt+Ctrl+S** to save changes as you go, without breaking the flow in your creativity. The file format must be RIFF, Painter's default format.

Take another close look at the pear and notice its texture, most apparent where the light shines obliquely but not directly on the fruit. To bring out that texture, we will use a strongly "grainy" variant, such as **Pastels > Round Hard Pastels**. First, choose a paper texture that imitates the pear's skin. It's not always easy to predict what a texture will look like just from the thumbnail swatches in the Paper Selector.

Test a few textures on a new canvas the same orange color as the pear drawing, using white with a **Hard Pastel** variant. The top row of Figure 2.6 shows three papers that won't work for this project: Pebble Board, Hard Laid Paper, and Course Cotton Canvas. Any of the bottom three papers will do nicely. They are, from left to right, Italian Watercolor, Rough Charcoal, and Charcoal Paper. With slightly vertical striations, Charcoal Paper is just about perfect. There is a custom palette for this project in the Palettes and Libraries folder on the CD, called Tonal Pear. It includes the paper swatch. Import it to your workspace with the **Custom Palette Organizer**.

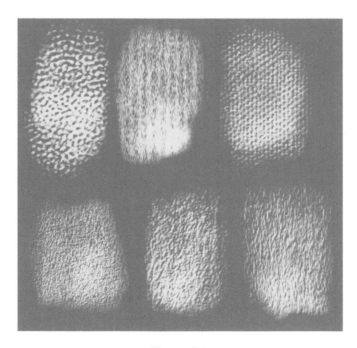

Figure 2.6
Papers, please!

Now that you have the outline, you don't really need tracing paper anymore, so turn it off and use the "eyeball" method—just look at the source photo to guide your placement of highlights and shadows. Apply a few white strokes with a **Hard Pastel** variant in the light areas, pressing harder in the brightest spots. Use the dark brown color from the outline to create the shadow areas. (Remember the modifier key for getting the Dropper function?) Try not to let white and brown strokes overlap or even touch each other, but rely on the paper color to express mid-tones. Only a few strokes are needed to bring out this voluptuous form. Refer to Figure 2.7 for guidance and encouragement.

Switch to the Conte stick to make a clean white edge where the light background meets the darkest part of the pear. Go back to Hard Pastel to add some white background on both sides of the pear, feathering out the edges with light pressure.

Figure 2.7
Easy does it—let the paper show through.

Figure 2.8 shows my completed drawing, with a few finishing touches. I added a small cast shadow under the pear. A couple of details on the stem were made with **Charcoal > Sharp Charcoal Pencil 5**, drawn in white and with the paper color. Finally, I gently removed some of the white outline on the lower left of the pear, allowing it to merge into the background. No need to switch to an Eraser variant for those last few strokes—use the other end of your Wacom pen!

Figure 2.8
A nice piece of fruit.

Are We There Yet?

How do you know where you're finished with a drawing or painting? If you've spent more than 15 minutes on this one, you're done! Trying to make your artwork perfect? Fuhgeddaboudit!

Cross-Hatch Contours

Let's take yet another close look at the pear. This time, concentrate on its rounded contours. We'll work on white paper with black lines. Tone and form will be built up from overlapping strokes that follow the contours of the pear. This is another traditional method, often used by cartoonists and graphic artists, especially for commercial black-and-white printing.

So, make another Quick Clone of the photo. Choose a thin pencil or pen that has little or no variation in thickness or opacity. I'm using the **2B Pencil**. Sketch the stem and right edge of the pear quickly, and begin to make a series of roughly parallel strokes that follow the curves of the fruit. Use strokes that vary in length and direction, building up the form. Your wrist will have to twist as you work. For darker areas, overlap strokes in different directions. This is similar to the warm-up cross-hatch exercise you did in Lesson 1— just a bit more controlled. Figure 2.9 shows the process, and the result can be very lively.

Figure 2.9

Are we pear, yet?

Don't Hurt Yourself

To keep from twisting your wrist too much, use Painter's cool **Rotate Paper** tool, available in all versions. It shares a space on the Toolbox with the **Grabber** hand, right next to the **Magnifier**. Figure 2.10 shows the tool active and the image tilted as desired. When you're ready to return to normal orientation, double-click the **Rotate Paper** tool.

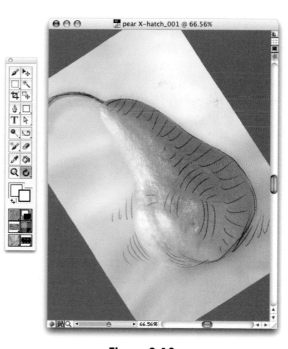

Figure 2.10

Let's do the twist!

Send in the Clones

If you've completed all the drawing exercises in this lesson, you've earned a treat. I don't mean eating the pear—but it was delicious (tossed with lettuce, celery, walnuts, and blue cheese dressing). No, I'm referring to Painter's incredible feature for turning photos into drawings and paintings, not by clicking on filter effects, but created one brush stroke at a time! And, yes, you're the one applying the brush strokes.

Taking Responsibility

Actually, you can get Painter to do all the work while you take a coffee break. Check the **Smart Stroke Brush** category, used in conjunction with the **Auto-Painting** palette. But that's not art—just a parlor trick. I use Painter to help me prepare an image and provide some shortcuts, but I reserve the right to make each stroke myself. Yes, that's where I really draw the line!

We've been using only the tracing paper feature of Cloning so far. You can turn any variant into a **Cloner Brush** by enabling **Clone Color** on the Color Picker. Its icon is a rubber stamp. Figure 2.11 shows **Clone Color** on, with the usual color selection area grayed out to indicate it's not available. For the current brush variant, then, all color information will be coming from the **Clone Source**. You'll see how this works in a minute.

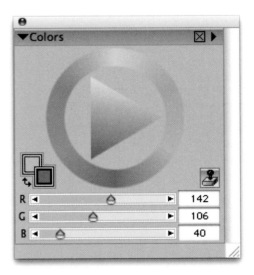

Figure 2.11
Color info will come from the Clone Source.

Let's make a clone drawing. Open the pear image again, and use the **Quick Clone** command. Choose **Pastels > Square Hard Pastels 10** and the Charcoal Paper texture used earlier. Enable **Clone Color** and apply strokes following the contour of the pear. (That's generally a good practice, whatever medium you use.) Make tracing paper more opaque as you go so you can see your work. Include a few strokes under the pear and in the background. Does your drawing look something like Figure 2.12? How cool is that?

Where Are the Clones?

Any brush variant can be made to function as a cloner, but there are dozens of "dedicated" cloners in the **Cloner Brush** category. You can jump to that category by choosing the **Cloner** tool in the Toolbox. **Cloner Brushes** have always been the most exciting feature of Painter, in my not so humble opinion.

Figure 2.12
Pastel clone drawing.

Pick a Pepper

If you'd like a change of pace, open one of the chili pepper photos from the Produce section of the source images on the CD. This pepper has such a fascinating shape that I took several shots of different "poses," some in bright sunlight and some indoors on a semi-gloss gray background—my Wacom tablet. Let's work with ChiliSunlit1.jpg, shown in Figure 2.13.

Figure 2.13

This is not a pear.

Painter X introduced a way to prepare an image to enhance the effectiveness of cloning, based on the style of clone you want to paint. These choices are found in the **Underpainting** palette, shown in Figure 2.14. I chose a new **Color Scheme** optimized for chalk drawing. The result, in Figure 2.15, has less saturated, warmer colors. Make a **Quick Clone** of this version and use **File > Save As** to choose the RIFF file format. Now you can preserve the stages of your drawing with **Iterative Save**.

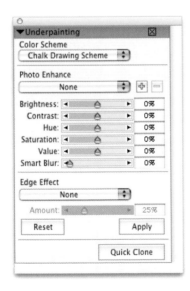

Figure 2.14

The Underpainting palette.

Figure 2.15

Prepared pepper.

This time we'll use an approach I call Scribble-Smear-Pick. There is a custom palette for this technique in the Palettes and Libraries folder on the CD. It includes my choice of texture, Sandy Pastel Paper. Import it now, or you can just select the variants I'm using and make your own custom palette:

- Pastels > Tapered Pastel 10

- Blenders > Pointed Stump 10

- Chalk > Sharp Chalk

Begin with the **Tapered Pastel** and **Clone Color** enabled. Make rough scribbles over most of the pepper, guided by the contours of the shape. Include the cast shadow and some of the background. The top image in Figure 2.16 shows this stage. Switch to the **Blender** and smooth out some (not all) of your scribbled strokes. Look closely at this stage with tracing paper turned off, comparing it to the source image. Decide which details you want to bring out. Pick out those details with **Sharp Chalk.**

Figure 2.16
Scribble, smear, and pick.

The final stage shows more detail on the stem and the small highlight on the upper part of the pepper near the stem. One very subtle but important element is the thin rim of reflection between the core shadow on the lower right of the pepper and the cast shadow. This could not easily be made with **Clone Color**, so I disabled that option, selected a light color, and drew it in with **Sharp Chalk**.

Repetitive Pepper

Prepare to make a pencil clone of the pepper. Go back to the original bright color scheme, and use a **Grainy Cover Pencil** variant, with Clone Color enabled. Try a technique similar to the cross-hatch contours you used on the pear (see Figure 2.10 again), allowing quite a bit of white paper to show through. Start with a quick outline of all the shapes, including the shadows.

Figure 2.17 shows the development of my pencil clone sketch. Notice the outlines around highlight shapes in the early stage. Playful scribbles are mixed with cross-hatching, building up tone in the shadows and darker parts of the pepper. Your sketch will have its own style and character—and spicy flavor.

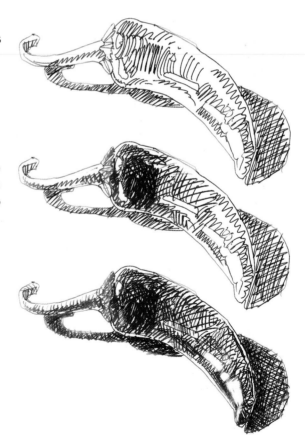

We'll return to cloning techniques in future lessons, but I just couldn't wait to introduce you to this powerful feature. No offense to the fabulous folks at Adobe Systems, but Painter's **Cloner Brushes** leave Photoshop in the dust!

Figure 2.17
Hot and spicy.

What's Next?

Keep practicing your tonal drawing and cross-hatch techniques, with or without the aid of **Clone Color**. There are source photos on the CD that came with this book to serve as subjects for drawing and painting at whatever your skill level. I also encourage you to go to the market and buy some nice fresh produce to work with. Make your own photos, but even better, set your hand-picked fruit or vegetable on a surface next to your computer and draw it live! Aim a spotlight on one side to get dramatic highlights and shadows. Figure 2.18 shows a basic setup.

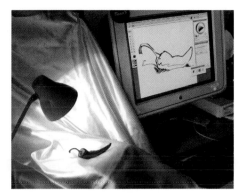

Figure 2.18
Chili pepper LIVE.

After every lesson or practice session, choose your best couple of drawings, or a series showing three or four stages in its development, and print them. That way you'll have tangible evidence of your work to hang on the walls. Over time you'll be able to observe your skills improving. Examining a print of your drawing is also a good way to evaluate it for possible changes.

Most desktop inkjet printers can create very high-quality output. To enhance the fine art nature of your image, use special paper or other media designed for your printer. High gloss heavy weight photo paper might be ideal for some projects, or canvas or watercolor paper for others. I printed my pencil clone pepper series on glossy photo paper for crisp lines and intense color. The chalk cloned peppers (Figure 2.17) are softer and more painterly, so I printed that series on a canvas sheet. (See the Appendix for resources.)

Drawing or Painting?

What's the difference? Sometimes not much, and we may use these terms interchangeably. In general, drawings are made with dry media, and paintings with wet. Or, if you render your subject mostly with lines, it's a drawing. But when tones and colors blend into each other without distinct edges, it's a painting. So, when you smeared the chalk lines on your pepper clone with a blender variant, did your drawing change into a painting? I'll let you decide. A traditional term for artwork composed with a variety of wet and dry materials, possibly incorporating photos or collage elements pasted on, is "mixed media." We'll be doing a lot of that.

Technically, everything you make in Painter is painting because it's done with pixels. Digital "drawing" requires a vector-based program like Illustrator. I'm glad I could clear that up.

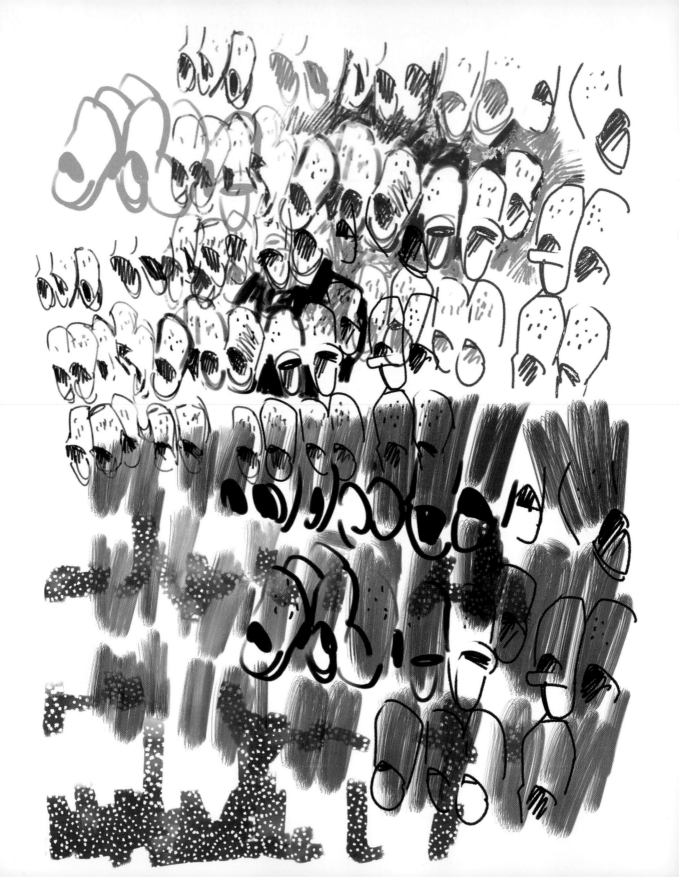

3 Working with Layers

Regardless of subject matter or style, it's often a good idea to separate elements of your artwork into layers. For example, draw outlines on one layer and create color on another. You'll be able to make changes to either layer while protecting the other.

The Chair

You'll see how layers work with a drawing of the leather chair and ottoman shown in Figure 3.1.

Open **leatherchair.jpg**, found in **Things > Furniture** on the CD that accompanies this book. Use **Canvas > Resize** if needed to fit the image on your screen. Make a **Quick Clone** to access the tracing paper feature. Choose a Pens variant that has some thick-and-thin response to pressure on your tablet but no variation in opacity. I suggest either the **Scratchboard** tool or **Croquil Pen 5.**

Working with black, make a loose sketch of the basic shapes, similar to Figure 3.2. Use heavier pressure to create stronger lines, such as the back of the seat cushion, or a lighter touch for seams and edges. Ignore most of the creases and folds for now—we'll use additional layers for that.

Figure 3.1
Pull up a chair.

Figure 3.2
Have a seat.

If you want to fix a line, no need to switch to the Eraser tool. Just use the Option/Alt key to get the Dropper function and click on the white background. Then "white out" the lines you want to correct. Press Option/Alt once again to click on a black pixel, and you're good to draw. I find my left thumb hovering over the modifier key as I work so I can change color quickly.

Add a Color Layer

We'll make a new layer for color. If you don't see the **Layers** palette on your workspace, launch it from the **Window** menu. Figure 3.3 shows where to click to create a new layer and where to change the **Composite Method** for determining how the layer will interact with the canvas image (or with other layers). The popup menu on the Layers palette has a New Layer command, or you can use the keyboard shortcut **Shift+Cmd/Ctrl+N**.

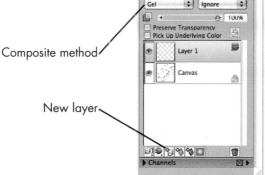

Composite method

New layer

Figure 3.3
Have another layer.

Sample a dusty rose color from the base of the ottoman. Choose **Pen > Flat Color** and begin to paint on the new layer. If your work looks like the left side of Figure 3.4, your layer is still using the **Default** composite method, and it is covering up your line drawing. To change that, switch to either **Gel** or **Multiply**.

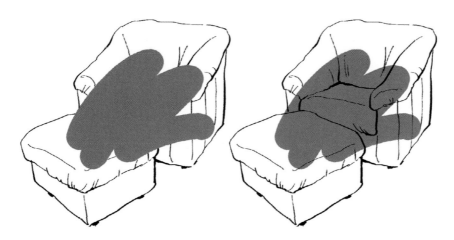

Figure 3.4
Composite method matters.

41

The **Flat Color** variant is too big for this project, so reduce its size with the left bracket ([) key or the Size slider in the **Property Bar** at the top of your workspace. Are you able to see a "ghost" image of the brush size when your Wacom pen hovers over the image? If not, you might want to **Enable Brush Ghosting** in **Preferences > General**. Paint flat color over the chair, as shown in Figure 3.5.

Speed vs. Visibility

Brush Ghosting shows the size and shape of the current brush as you hover the pen over your canvas. **Enhanced Brush Ghosting** even shows the tilt of your pen, but there can be a downside to that. If you're using a complex brush, such as a **RealBristle** variant, and your computer is older or less powerful than the latest models, the result is slower brush action. When that happens, just turn off **Enhanced Brush Ghosting**.

Figure 3.5

Flat finish.

Add Tone and Texture

To protect the flat color layer, you'll need additional layers for highlights and shadows. Make two new layers and rename each of them so you can keep track of what goes where. Change the name of a layer by double-clicking on it in the list and typing whatever you like in the **Layer Attributes** dialog box. Figure 3.6 shows my Layers palette at this stage.

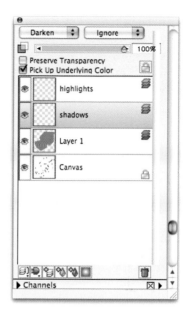

Use a slightly darker color for painting the shadows. A quick way to alter the value (brightness) or saturation (purity) of a color is with the triangle inside the Hue ring of the Colors palette. Figure 3.7 shows the Colors palette with our basic chair color on the left and the new darker color on the right. Just drag the indicator down a bit to reduce the Value from 139 to 109. For more precision, type the new value into the V field. It helps to change the display from RGB to HSV. You'll find that option in the popup menu of the Colors palette.

Figure 3.6
Layer stack.

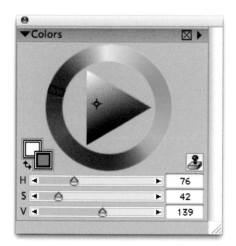 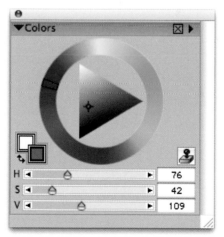

Figure 3.7
Changing values.

With Basic Paper (or whatever texture you prefer), use a grainy Chalk or Pastel variant to stroke in some darker areas on the shadow layer. I used **Square Hard Pastel 25**. The original photo has light coming from the upper right, so use that for reference. Your image should look similar to Figure 3.8 if you switched the composite method to Darken.

There's Method to My Method

If you're not sure why the Darken method works best for this situation, try switching back to Default and notice that the shadow color hides the black line drawing. Not good. Now try the Gel or Multiply method. Black lines show okay, but now the shadow color is combined with the flat color and is too dark. Not good. The Darken method compares the two layers and always lets the darker pixel win. So, black line wins over shadow color, and shadow color wins over basic flat color. Good.

Figure 3.8

Not so flat.

Consider a couple of ways to handle the Highlights layer. You could apply chalk or pastel strokes with a slightly brighter rose color, using the Default composite method. Pointed Eraser 7 will reveal the black lines again. That Eraser variant can also reveal areas of the base color to render creases in the leather. A detail on the left in Figure 3.9 shows the results.

The other two close-ups show a different approach. I wanted to find a way to let the black lines show through while painting lighter strokes over the base color. Finding the right combination of color and composite method for the Highlights layer is an interesting challenge. Explore on your own before you peek at the next sentence.

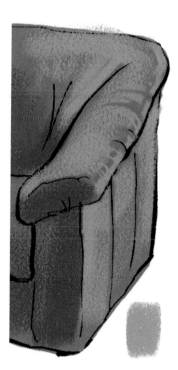
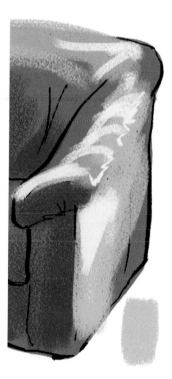
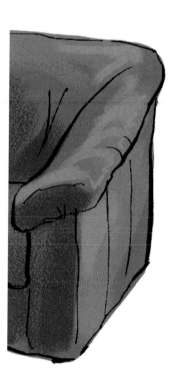

Figure 3.9
Details, details!

The solution is to paint with very bright light pink and pure white, using the **Soft Light** composite method. If you found another way to do it, great! The center detail shows the Highlights layer fully opaque (the Default method). The finished chair in Figure 3.10 had some edges softened with the **Smudge** variant in the **Blender** category. Some interior black lines on the original canvas were no longer needed, so they were erased.

Always keep the layered RIFF files in case you want to continue working on your image. To flatten your composite and save as a JPEG or in another file format, use the **Drop All** command in the **Layers** popup menu. More info on file formats can be found in the Appendix.

Figure 3.10

Sit down and relax.

Loose Shoes

Open the photo **Crocs_shoes.jpg** from the source images folder on the CD that accompanies this book. We'll create a playful painting loosely based on these loose-fitting (and silly looking) shoes. Choose **Impressionist Scheme** from the **Color Scheme** list in the **Underpainting** palette. Figure 3.11 shows that the result keeps most of the saturated color while bringing some detail out of the deep shadows. We'll make separate layers for color and outlines, as with the leather chair project, but we'll use very different styles and techniques. First save the image as a RIFF file so you can make iterative saves quickly as you work.

Figure 3.11
What a Croc!

Quick Color and Line

Select **File > Quick Clone** and choose **Smeary Bristle Cloner** from the **Cloners** category. Make splashes of color on the new canvas, using mostly vertical scribbles on each shoe shape, similar to Figure 3.12.

Make a new layer for outline work. With either **Pointed Crayon 7** or **Thick n Thin Marker 10** (from the **Felt Pens** group), sketch the basic lines and curves for each shoe shape in black, working freely and without concern for accuracy or detail. This style can be called loose, rough, or "quick n dirty." Adjust tracing paper opacity to taste, and toggle it off frequently to see your work. Figure 3.13 shows this stage, including several pink and yellow shoes on the left, which are using **Clone Color** instead of black for the line work.

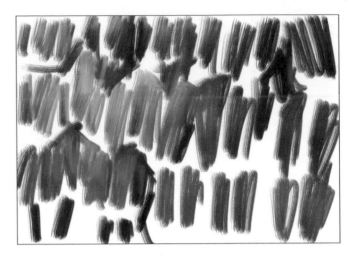

Figure 3.12
Smeary Bristle color.

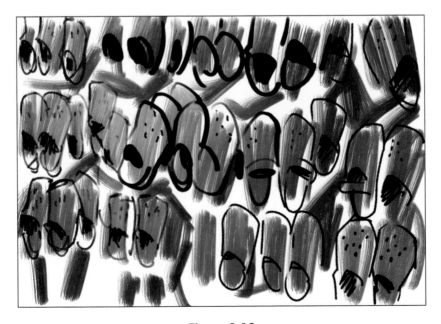

Figure 3.13
Dark lines added.

Some parts of this painting are working better than others. Erase and redo some lines, but don't get too picky. Figure 3.14 shows only the line layer at this point, with some extra scribbling for a darker focal point. Crayon and Marker lines can get very dark, even when using **Clone Color**, because they use the **Buildup** brush method. Toggle the visibility of any layer (or the canvas itself) with the eyeball icons in the Layers palette.

Figure 3.14
Lines layer only.

Textured Background

The painting needs something to tie the elements together. A pattern of dots to echo the perforations on the shoes is worth a try. Let's add another layer for applying grainy strokes with a Square Hard Pastel. We'll need to find just the right paper. Use File > New to make a new canvas for testing textures. Fine Dots from the default paper library is a good candidate. Launch the palette and increase the size of the texture to about 200%. The first swatch on the left in Figure 3.15 was made with these not-so-fine dots. I used the **Invert Paper** command in the Papers palette popup (can you say that without spitting?) menu to make a negative version for the second swatch.

fine dots
resized to 200%

fine dots
inverted

Fuzzy
Confetti

Fuzzy Confetti
resized to 200%

Fuzzy Confetti
inverted and
high contrast

Figure 3.15

Texture tester.

The dots should be more scattered and irregular in order to maintain the casual style of this piece. We could easily make a custom paper texture from scratch, but let's open another library first. The popup menu on the **Paper Selector** has an **Open Library** command for browsing and loading alternative collections of papers. Use it to replace the current library with **Crazy Textures**. You should find a couple of dozen paper libraries in the Extras folder wherever your Painter application is making its home on your computer hard drive. **Fuzzy Confetti** looks very promising when enlarged. Figure 3.16 shows my settings for changing the size, contrast, and brightness of the paper. Notice that a toggle button for inverting paper is available here as well as in the popup menu.

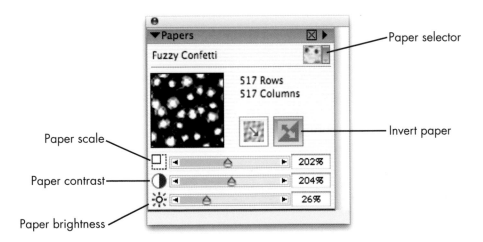

Figure 3.16

Fat bright confetti.

Bold strokes with the **Square Hard Pastel** were applied to most of the spaces between shoes on the new layer. I did not invert the paper after all in order to get more color coverage. The dots reveal background white (or black in some areas). Use **Clone Color** to achieve more color harmony with the other layers. The composite at this stage is shown in Figure 3.17.

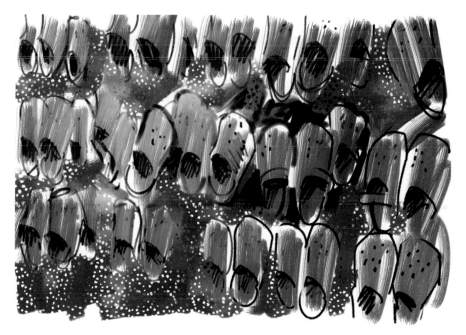

Figure 3.17
If the shoes fit.

Step Back

When you're not trying for realism, it's harder to know when you're done. "Real life" painters often step back to look at their artwork from a distance to get the big picture. You'll see the art better if you eliminate screen clutter. Press the Tab key to make all open palettes disappear (press again when you want to see them). Another handy toggle is **Screen Mode (Cmd/Ctrl+M)**, which makes all open windows invisible. The current image will be surrounded by a neutral gray, which is best for judging how your colors look.

Organize Your Papers

As long as we're on a break, let's do some paper work. There's no need to load several different libraries in search of a special paper texture after you create your own custom libraries with the **Paper Mover.** (A Mover utility is available for each resource in the content selector area—Gradients, Patterns, Weaves, Looks, and Nozzles.)

Choose **Paper Mover** from the popup menu on the **Paper Selector.** The **Paper Mover** dialog box opens, with thumbnail swatches of all the items in the current library displayed on the left. There is an empty area on the right. To start a new collection, click the New button and give your library a name. Now you can drag items from the default collection to your new one. Figure 3.18 has some of my favorite papers dragged over to my new custom library. I can add items from other libraries by using the Open/Close toggle button commands on the left side.

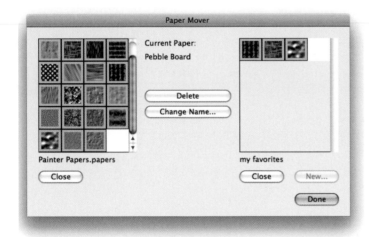

Figure 3.18
Get your papers in order.

Make Your Own Paper

A paper texture in Painter is simply a rectangular grayscale image that repeats as a seamless tile. You can start a new paper tile by making a brush stroke to select, you can fill a small rectangle with several brush strokes, or you can drag a rectangular selection in an existing image. Let's do all three.

Select **File > New** to make a plain white canvas for creating and testing new paper textures. About 600 pixels square is fine, at any resolution. Make a small diagonal squiggle with the **Thick n Thin Pen** and drag a rectangular selection marquee around it, as shown in the left portion of Figure 3.19.

Figure 3.19
Squiggle, scribbles, and beans.

Find the **Capture Paper** command in the popup menu for either the **Paper Selector** or the **Papers** palette. You'll be prompted to name your new paper, and it will instantly become part of the current library. Test the new **Diagonal Squiggle** paper (or whatever you called it) with a **Hard Pastel** variant, changing the scale and inverting the values for different looks.

The center section of Figure 3.19 was made by scribbling with the **Nervous Pen**, a jittery variant in the **Pens** category. Finally, there is an example of making a paper texture from a photo of coffee beans, found in the Source Images folder on the CD that accompanies this book. The procedure was the same for all three: select, capture, and name. Figure 3.20 has tests of all three new papers. The two-tone effect for the coffee beans was made by inverting the paper and painting over the same area with a different color. Use the **Paper Mover** to organize your custom papers into a unique library and to delete the ones you never want to see again.

Figure 3.20
Three new papers.

Gotcha!

Don't confuse the **Make Paper** command with the **Capture Paper** command. Make Paper lets you produce a texture from a small list of geometric elements, such as lines or squares. Capture Paper requires making a selection on any open image and is much more fun. The "capture" feature is also available for making new brush tips and patterns. Anything you can surround with the marching ants of a selection marquee is up for "grabs!"

Finishing Touches

We've had our coffee break, literally, so it's back to the shoe painting. I admit that I had no clear idea where I was headed with this piece. This is just the kind of adventure I enjoy—plunging into unknown territory with very little chance of physical injury! Looking at it again with fresh eyes, there are some choices to consider. These are your alternatives at any stage in creating a layered painting:

- Add more to a layer

- Erase parts of a layer

- Reduce a layer's opacity

- Change the composite method of a layer

- Change the stacking order of layers

- Add another layer

I thought the dark area on the line layer was a bit harsh, so I added more crayon strokes (with Clone Color), to extend it and feather the edges somewhat, as shown in Figure 3.21. I was satisfied. Well, not quite. Switching back and forth among several composite methods, I found the combination in Figure 3.22 worth saving as an alternative version. The texture layer is now in Multiply mode, which changes the value (light and dark) distribution, especially with the line layer in Color mode. In this version the darkest areas become brilliant saturated color!

Figure 3.21
Finished line layer.

So Many Haystacks … So Little Time!

Claude Monet, the great Impressionist painter of the late nineteenth century, spent over a year making 25 paintings of haystacks at different times of day and different seasonal conditions. Can you imagine how much more productive he could've been using layers and composite methods?

Figure 3.22
And the runner-up is. . .

What's Next?

You've had a taste of layers, enough to demonstrate how powerful they can be in the development of a painting. You explored composite methods (same as Photoshop's blending modes) and learned to capture paper texture elements from just about anywhere.

In upcoming chapters, you'll begin to work with brush controls to understand the anatomy of a brush and how to bend it to your will.

4 The Great Outdoors

So far we've worked with simple objects—food, furniture, and footwear. Let's take on more complex subject matter, such as landscapes and street scenes. No need to actually be exposed to the elements or the prying eyes (and harsh criticism) of tourists. We'll work from photographs. Later on, though, you're encouraged to pack a lunch with your laptop and set out for digital plein aire painting in the park.

Landscape

Open **5_trees.jpg,** shown in Figure 4.1 and found in the Nature folder on the CD. Let's look closely at it to plan our strategy.

The Big Picture

The first thing to do with a complex subject is—simplify it. Traditional artists have a great low-tech way to reduce detail and just see a composition of light and shadow. It's called *squinting*. When you do that, you'll see past the individual branches and notice that the entire upper half of the image is mostly dark, with just a few patches of light as "negative shapes." The bottom one-third is, basically, a midtone that visually anchors the strong vertical dark shapes. For me, the most intriguing areas are the very bright negative shapes between the tree trunks. They also make a bold horizontal band in contrast with the dark vertical shapes.

Figure 4.1

Trees a crowd.

Combining some techniques used in earlier lessons, you'll paint both with and without Clone Color, and you'll use tinted paper. The first stage in our painting will simplify shapes and minimize detail. Later, we'll add selected details like a few bits of sky showing through tree branches and patches of sunlight on the grass.

Color Settings and Sets

Before we start painting, let's try a new **Color Scheme** from the **Underpainting** palette. I like the **Classical Color Scheme**, shown in Figure 4.2. That chocolate brown looks yummy, and there is now less detail in the branches, an unexpected benefit. This image is provided in the Nature folder, as **5_trees_ClassicalCS.jpg,** for users of Painter IX or earlier.

Find and open the **Color Sets** palette, a member of the Colors palette group. Clicking on a swatch in the Color Set is an alternative to finding and changing your main color for drawing and painting. A wide variety of Color Sets can be loaded from the Support files in your Painter application folder. A great way to access all the available colors in an image is to create a Color Set from the image.

Choose **New Color Set from Image** in the **Color Sets** popup menu. It will be useful sooner or later, and probably both. This new Color Set, shown in Figure 4.3, might look a bit different from yours until you change the way color swatches are displayed. I chose a slightly larger swatch size, 8×16 pixels. I also changed the sort order to LHS so that the swatches are arranged primarily according to Lightness (L). You can have them sorted by Hue (H) or Saturation (S), whatever makes more visual sense to you.

Sample a medium olive green from the Color Sets palette. (See, it was useful sooner than you thought.) Choose **Canvas > Set Paper Color**. Create a **Quick Clone**—can you guess what the background color will be?

Figure 4.2
Classical trees.

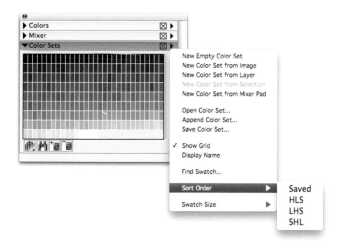

Figure 4.3
Classical colors.

Pick a Paper Color

When you start a new canvas, there is a white swatch showing the default paper color. Click it for several ways to choose a different background color. Figure 4.4 shows choosing a color based on its red, green, and blue components. That magnifier icon should probably be an eyedropper because it lets you sample a color anywhere on your monitor. You can use the Image palette to open a thumbnail of any image on your hard drive. In Figure 4.5, I'm sampling a gold color from a Monet haystack painting.

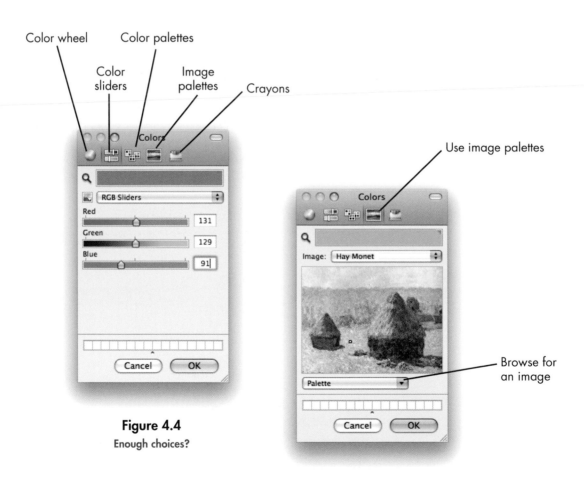

Figure 4.4

Enough choices?

Figure 4.5

Hey, Monet!

Tool Marks

Let's use **Oil Pastel** for this painting. It will produce smooth, creamy strokes. Notice that Oil Pastel variants come in different tip shapes. I like the **Chunky** group with an elliptical tip, but you might prefer round, rectangular, or triangle-shaped tips. Size is more important than shape for the preliminary painting. At a 30-pixels size, using **Clone Color**, you can "rough in" the basic tree trunks and major branches with very few strokes. Figure 4.6 shows this stage, with tracing paper on.

Figure 4.6
Roughing it.

Size and Detail

When you paint with Clone Color, the bigger your brush, the less detail you will get. In general, you'll want to begin with a large brush size for the broad strokes. Details can be created later with smaller size brush tips.

Continue painting the upper section of the image with a 30-pixel Oil Pastel, using directional strokes that follow the main branches. Most of the dark upper section of the trees will have no detail at all, just some color variation. Use shorter strokes in a variety of directions to fill that area. Figure 4.7 shows how fresh and lively this can look. Don't try to make your work look exactly like mine, and don't bother to undo strokes you don't like. Paint right over them—just like in real life!

The same basic technique works well on the grass and that strip of trees in the background. You are deliberately eliminating details, but not variety. Don't make your brush strokes too smooth. Figure 4.8 is developing nicely.

Figure 4.7
Fresh paint.

Figure 4.8
Rough enough.

Artistic License

That bright horizontal strip I like so much is practically pure white, and I think it will look too harsh if we clone it in. Let's turn off Clone Color and choose a lemony yellow from the color set. Paint those negative shapes in the same rough style we've been using. At this point I created a soft edge for the painting to blend with the paper color. That is done automatically with another cool feature on the **Underpainting** palette. It's the **Jagged Vignette** on the **Edge Effects** menu. Turn the default 25% down to about 10% to make the edge this narrow. Figure 4.9 shows the sunny yellow strip and the vignette edge.

Let's soften some of the edges inside the painting, too. Switch to a **Blender** for that purpose. I used the **Soft Blender Stump 20** to gently smooth and smear over some of the harsh color transitions.

We're ready to bring in some details now, bright patches of sky and grass. Using a smaller Oil Pastel, at about 20 pixels, dab on some spots of color, using tracing paper for reference if needed. We expect sky to be blue, but there isn't any sky blue in the Color Set. There's no law against going outside the Color Set, but I found some pinkish tones that worked out fine. Figure 4.10 has these bright spots added and softened a bit with the Blender Stump.

Figure 4.9
Soften the edges.

Figure 4.10
A few bright spots.

> ## You fill Up My Screen
>
> Working with a large image? Make the most of your screen space with **Screen Mode** toggle (**Cmd/Ctrl+M**). Visibility of all palettes can be toggled with the Tab key. Make zooming and scrolling easy with keyboard controls. The **spacebar** gives you the grabber, while **spacebar+Cmd/Ctrl** lets you click to zoom in. Add the **Option/Alt** key to that combination for zooming out. It's important to look at your image at 100% magnification fairly often, as some textures and effects look weird otherwise. Double-click the **Magnifier** tool to get 100% size instantly.

Cityscape

If you're an urban dweller, the cluster of Victorian houses in Figure 4.11 might seem as natural as a group of trees. We'll begin this new project with some attention to cropping and composition. Painter X introduced a feature for composing and placing the focal point of an image according to the classical Golden Rectangle (about 3:5 ratio). The Divine Proportion grid is an aid for cropping and finding the center of interest that was aesthetically pleasing to the Renaissance eye, and it still works today.

City Planning

Choose **Show Divine Proportion** from the **Window** menu and click the **Enable Divine Proportion** check box. Our image is vertical, so we need to pick one of the **Portrait** orientation formats. The focal point for this painting, in my judgment, is the area where the two main roofs and the power pole intersect. This is in the upper right quadrant, so choose the **Portrait** (**bottom left**) orientation, as shown in Figure 4.12. You'll need to use the **Divine Proportion** tool in the **Toolbox** (its icon is the same as the orientation curves) to move the grid to the position you want. The **Size** and **Rotate** sliders in the palette let you fit the grid to your image.

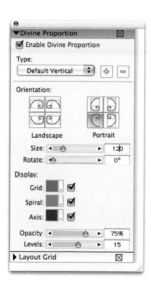

Figure 4.12
How divine!

Figure 4.11
Street of San Francisco.

When I place the "divine focal point" where I want it, the result is shown in Figure 4.13. Opacity of the photo was reduced so you could see the grid better. I'd like to crop out (or just ignore) the cars and the dark shape on the right. When we reduce the size of the grid to about 80% and reposition the focal point, the left and bottom edges look fine, but we lose the top of the power pole, which I'd like to keep as a secondary area of interest. Let's shorten the pole just a little. No, it's not cheating—it's image manipulation.

Drag a rectangular selection around the upper part of the photo, as shown in Figure 4.14. Click inside the selection with the **Layer Adjuster** tool, which "floats" the selection and makes it into a new layer. Now move the layer down to the position shown in Figure 4.15. Part of the roof is hidden by the layer. Fix that by changing the composite method to Darken. Use the **Drop** command in the **Layers** palette popup menu to flatten the image.

Figure 4.14
Rectangular selection.

Figure 4.13
You look divine!

Layer covers
part of roof

Lower edge
of layer

Figure 4.15
Assume the position.

We're almost ready to crop the photo. Let's add some white paper at the left edge for wiggle room. Select **Canvas > Canvas Size** with the settings shown in Figure 4.16. This command does not change the size of the image—it just adds extra pixels around the edges.

Canvas Size	
Current Size:	
Width: 987	pixels
Height: 1600	pixels
Adjust Size:	
Add: 0	pixels to top
Add: 100	pixels to left
Add: 0	pixels to bottom
Add: 0	pixels to right
	Cancel OK

Figure 4.16
Enlarge the canvas.

If everything looks perfect, use the **Crop** tool to drag from one corner of the **Divine Proportion** grid to the opposite diagonal corner and click inside the image to apply the crop. Well, things are hardly ever perfect, so I cheated once again to get the "not-quite-divine" cropped photo in Figure 4.17. Those extra white pixels on the left may come in handy.

If that seemed like an awful lot of preparation before you even make the first brush stroke, think how much time and effort it would take to stretch and prepare a traditional canvas!

Figure 4.17

Nearly divine.

Lay the Foundation

Once again, this will be a layered project, with a watercolor layer for color and a pencil sketch for lines and details. You'll also make a preliminary layout on its own layer, which you can throw in the digital trashcan after it serves its purpose. Start by making a **Quick Clone** of your cropped photo. Click on the **New Layer** icon three times and name the layers "color," "sketch," and "layout." Double-clicking on a layer brings up the **Layer Attributes** dialog with the name field ready for a change. Stacking order of the layers doesn't matter for now and can be changed at any time by dragging layers up or down in the palette. Use the **Gel** or **Multiply** composite method for all layers so they can be transparent with each other. That's so important in any relationship.

There are quite a few straight lines in this image, but don't let that scare you. We won't even try to do an architecturally accurate rendering. Help is available, however, if you need something to steady your hand. Any brush can be used in **Freehand** mode (the default) or **Straight Line** mode. Click on the icon for the function you want in the Property Bar along the upper edge of your screen. The Property Bar is context sensitive, meaning it changes according to the tool you are using. Figure 4.18 shows the controls available for the Brush tool. (Some brush categories offer a slightly different set of control variables.)

Current tool   Straight line

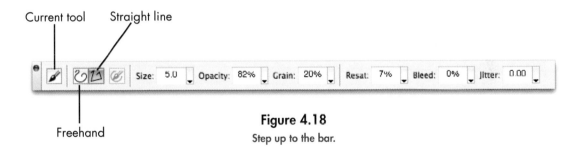

Freehand

Figure 4.18
Step up to the bar.

Property Values

The **Grain** setting is available for variants that show paper texture. A lower setting produces a stronger texture. This seems counterintuitive, until you understand that lower values reduce penetration into the grain, while higher values increase penetration. Complete penetration (100% Grain) is no texture at all! **Resat** means *resaturation* and refers to the amount of color replenished in the stroke. **Blender** variants do not add color at all, but only smear existing color, so they have a Resat setting of zero. **Bleed** refers to the amount of mixing with underlying color, so you can expect Blenders to have relatively high values for Bleed.

With the 3- and 5-pixel size Sketching Pencil in Straight Line mode, sketch out some of the important lines on your layout layer in black or brown. Figure 4.19 shows my layout. Key commands for switching between Freehand and Straight Line mode are "b" and "v"—easy to remember because of their shapes, and because they are next to each other on the keyboard. You'll want to use them instead of the Property Bar for quick changes between modes. When creating a drawing with mostly straight lines, press "b" then "v" before you begin a new line at a different point. Otherwise, all your lines will be connected.

Figure 4.19
Line power.

Just Add Water

The colors in the photo are much too dull, so we won't use Clone Color. There is a Color Set that is ideal for this piece. Use the **Open Color Set** command in the **Color Sets** palette and choose **Muted Tones** from the Support files in your Painter application folder. Figure 4.20 shows this Color Set with 24×24 pixels swatch size and HLS sort order. I wanted to be able to see the swatches organized mainly by hue (H).

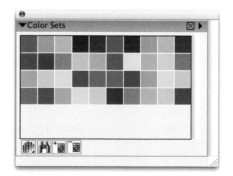

Figure 4.20
Quiet colors.

We'll use **Digital Watercolor** variants on the color layer. Splash around with several variants to get the hang of them. Change the size of a brush with your bracket keys or the Size slider in the Property Bar. Be sure to try Spatter Water and Salt, as well as some Blender variants in the Digital Watercolor category. Figure 4.21 shows some experimentation.

Notice that the Property Bar for Digital Watercolor brushes has sliders for Diffusion and Wet Fringe. Diffusion reveals paper texture, so choose a paper that will enhance your strokes. Wet Fringe refers to the pooling of pigment at the outer edge of a stroke, a distinctive quality of watercolor painting. Try changing the Diffusion or Wet Fringe values and see how your brush strokes are affected.

Figure 4.21
Just practice.

Soft and Hard Water

Traditional watercolor effects are perhaps the most difficult to emulate, but Painter lets you come very close. The brushes in the **Digital Watercolor** category are easier to work with than the more advanced **Watercolor**, which requires its own special layer. Play with variants from both categories to compare them.

Either delete the experimental scribbles from the color layer or just make them invisible and create a new layer for more "serious" color work. With your layout or tracing paper (or both) as a guide, paint a color layer using broad strokes. My effort is shown in Figure 4.22. I worked in Freehand mode mostly, but I used Straight Line strokes for the power pole. The layout layer, hidden for now, helped me keep things simple. I am more concerned with getting the light and dark values of the photo correct than the color hues.

Figure 4.22

Simple color.

Default Lies Not in Our Stars...

All changes you make to a variant will remain until you deliberately restore the original settings, using the aptly named **Restore Default Variant** command in the **Brush Selector Bar** popup menu. If you tweak a bunch of controls and come up with a really great custom brush that you don't want to lose, play it safe and use the **Save Variant** command, giving your special brush a unique name. It will take its place alphabetically in the current brush category.

We'll make another layer (or two) for details. Use a smaller brush, such as **Fine Tip Water**, to paint in some of the details on the left half of the image, as shown in Figure 4.23. I dabbed on the Victorian "gingerbread" trim in dark red and teal blue, mixing Freehand with Straight Line strokes. I needed to reduce the size of the brush for some of the straight lines. That's because Straight Line mode doesn't allow for pressure variations, giving you the brush at full strength.

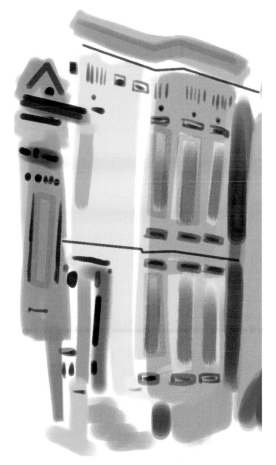

Figure 4.23
Victorian ornamentation.

All the Trimmings

The layout layer should stay hidden from this point on, but don't dump it—it could come in handy later. It's finally time to work on the "sketch" layer. We'll use a fine tip pen or pencil for black line details. In keeping with the style of the piece, continue to mix free-hand with straight lines. Draw important and interesting details, leaving out stuff you don't need. Hide and reveal the color layers and tracing paper as needed to see how your work is progressing. You can zoom in and out with Cmd/Ctrl and the plus or minus key. Use the **Rotate Page** tool (sharing a small studio apartment with the **Grabber**) when you want to tilt the canvas to another position.

I used **Sharp Colored Pencil 5** and **3** with several dark colors for the sketch layer shown in Figure 4.24. Figure 4.25 shows my final composite. It even includes the preliminary layout layer, using the **Hard Light** composite method. Never throw anything away! All the stages in this project are included on the CD, so you can examine and experiment with them. There's more I could do with this, but according to my watch I'm due in the next chapter. Okay, just one more thing—some wacky color variations made in a jiffy with **Effect's > Tonal Control > Adjust Colors**. When the **Adjust Colors** dialog appears, move the **Hue Shift** slider and choose **Paper** in the **Using** field instead of **Uniform Color**. My results can be found in the lower right section of the illustration at the beginning of this chapter. Incidentally, the caption "Painted ladies" is a reference to a book of photos of some of the more outrageously colorful Victorian buildings in San Francisco.

Figure 4.24
Sketchy.

Figure 4.25
Painted ladies.

What's Next?

Well, that's enough fresh air for one day. Let's go back indoors.

You have tackled increasingly complex subjects, and you are probably developing more confidence with Painter's tools and features. At least you're willing to take more risks. You had your first taste of Painter's special effects, and you got to nibble the edges of Brush Controls. There are many more variables influencing brush behavior (and flavor) than you see on the Property Bar—enough to satiate any control freak, and more than enough to give the rest of us—well, a tummy ache.

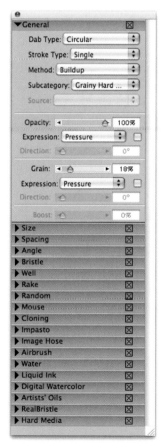

The **Brush Controls** palette shown in Figure 4.26 is actually a group of palettes, with sections that are more or less useful, depending on the category of brush you're working with. The General controls section is expanded here. You might never use some of these sections, and you certainly won't need to have more than a few showing at one time. Customize any palette group by closing the sections you don't need: Just click the X-box.

When you have a sense of which palettes you want access to, place them exactly the way you want them and hide the rest. Use **Window > Arrange Palettes > Save Layout** to name the arrangement for easy access. Have different palette layouts for special projects—one for sketching, another for clone painting from a photo, and so on.

Painter X and **Painter 11** let you customize every aspect of the program and save them all as a workspace. Yes, you can have several workspace arrangements for different projects or techniques. You can export a workspace to another hard drive or import the workspaces of other users. There are some that came with your Painter program discs. If you want to see how John Derry works (he's one of the original creators of Painter) or look over the freckled shoulder of Cher Threinen-Pendarvis (author of the *Painter WOW!* series), import their workspaces. It might not make you more creative, but it couldn't hurt.

Figure 4.26
I got your brush controls right here!

5 Painting People

Drawing and painting the human face and form provides a much greater challenge than scenes and still lifes. (Or is it "still lives"?) If your hand slips when you're drawing an apple or a chair, it's not a problem. But a tiny little mistake when you're working on a portrait, and suddenly, he's not your Uncle Ira anymore! Also, when you're sketching a still life, your subject is unlikely to insist you "make my stem smaller," or complain "am I really that green?"

So, accuracy and proportion are important for drawing the human face and figure. There are basic principles, whatever our subject: Choose a composition, simplify the forms, and then develop enough details to engage the viewer. One or more of those principles can be bent in service of expressing a viewpoint, a feeling, or in search of a personal style. However, we always have the same fundamental elements to work with: lines, shapes, tonality (light and shadow), and texture.

Colorful Portrait

Portraiture is a particular passion of mine. I often experiment with vibrant colors, in both my traditional and digital work. Painter has many tools and features to add brilliant hues to ho-hum realism. You've already used the Color Scheme selector in the Underpainting palette. We'll look into more options for altering color in this chapter.

Work with a photo of someone you don't know so you're not influenced by your feelings for (or against) the person. It's a good idea to avoid young children (their faces aren't developed yet) and exceptionally good-looking people (so many reasons, including damage to your self-esteem). Find the photo you want to work with, or join me in using **Audrey.jpg**, shown in Figure 5.1 and available on the CD in the Lesson 5 folder.

Figure 5.1
Audrey photo.

Ramp It Up

The photo will be used as a Clone Source for part of this project, so we need to manipulate the colors before we begin painting. An intriguing way to add wild color effects is to apply a **Gradient** color ramp to the image. Choose **Vivid Mixture** from the **Gradient Selector** next to the Paper Selector at the bottom of the Toolbox, as shown in Figure 5.2. Use the **Express in Image** command in the popup menu. You'll need to adjust the **Bias** slider, as shown in Figure 5.3, to map the values of the gradient to the values of your image. The preview thumbnail shows changes in value mapping as you move the slider around. I wanted to maintain the original distribution of values for the result shown in Figure 5.4.

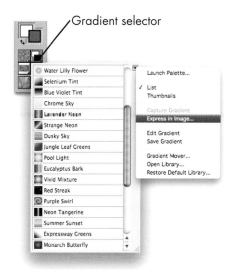

Figure 5.2

Select a gradient.

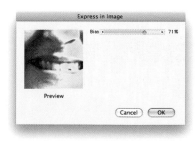

Figure 5.3

How biased are you?

Figure 5.4

Vivid mix.

With a bias around 43%, you'll get an effect reminiscent of sixties psychedelic art. Figure 5.5 shows this solarization effect at full strength on the left and after the **Edit > Fade** command was used to restore 50% of the previous state. It's still pretty wacky.

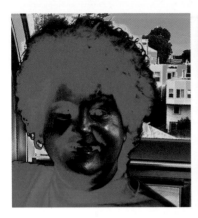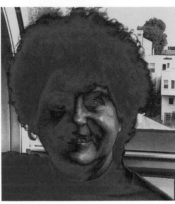

Figure 5.5

Far out and near out.

---

fading fast

Don't rush to undo an effect or a brushstroke just because it's too strong or too opaque. Use Edit > Fade to tone it down by any percentage you choose.

There are several collections of gradients you can load to replace the default library, just as you can with paper textures. It might be quicker to make your own custom gradient with the **Edit Gradient** command in the palette popup menu. I'll demonstrate by editing Neon Tangerine. (Weren't they a rock band in the seventies?) Figure 5.6 shows both the Gradients palette and the Edit Gradient dialog. The little gray triangles along the bottom edge of the color ramp are color control points. To add a new color, click on a control point and choose a color from your color palette. Slide the control point left or right to adjust the way colors blend. If you need another control point, click where you want it to appear.

Figure 5.6
Ready to edit.

When you're done editing, click OK and be sure to use the **Save Gradient** command if you want to add it to your current library. I named the gradient shown in Figure 5.7 orange-red-purple and applied it to the Audrey photo with the Express in Image command. I faded the effect by 50% for the version shown in Figure 5.8. This will be my new Clone Source.

Figure 5.7
Custom gradient.

Figure 5.8
Audrey ready.

Smear It Up

Select **File > Clone** to make a copy of the image. Don't use Quick Clone this time, because we don't want the copy deleted. We'll use a smeary variant to blend edges, wipe out details, and create interesting brushstrokes. The Coarse Oily Blenders in the Blender category let you make wonderful juicy smears by pulling color around. Experiment with this variant by filling a new canvas with a multicolored gradient so you can observe the behavior of the brush as you drag it across different colors. Figure 5.9 shows several long squiggles that pick up color at the beginning of a stroke and continue to smear that color for the length of the stroke. You can take advantage of that fact when you work. Short strokes work best to create variety and a layering of color.

Figure 5.9

Smear me once, shame on you!

Testing Brushes

Before you begin working with a brush category or variant that's unfamiliar to you, create a new document for testing it under a variety of situations: Paint over different backgrounds using different colors, pressure, and direction. Make some long strokes to see if pigment fades out. Drag a stroke over changing colors to observe the smeariness of the brush. See what happens when you change the value of controls in the Property Bar, then use **Restore Default Variant** in the Brush Selector Bar menu.

There is a custom palette for this project on the CD that accompanies this book. It's called Impasto Smear and includes all three sizes of Coarse Oily Blenders. I used the 30-pixel size for the background, and smaller sizes for Audrey's hair and face. A couple of minutes spent splashing around led me to the stage in Figure 5.10.

Yes, I messed up her eyes and mouth a little too much. Not a problem with a pristine version standing by as a Clone Source "safety net." Use the **VanGogh Cloner** to bring back some detail to the face or other areas you want to redo so you can apply the smears more effectively. The VanGogh variant is an ideal choice of cloner for this situation. It has multiple strokes similar to the look of the Coarse Oily Blenders. The detail in Figure 5.11 shows how nicely they can work (and play) together.

Figure 5.10
Coarse and oily.

Figure 5.11
Oily and Vinnie.

Fluff It Up

Let's add some thick paint effects to Audrey's mop of curly hair. Painter has a whole category of brushes devoted to Impasto (thick paint) brushes and techniques. Make short, curved strokes with the **Smeary Varnish** variant. If you want to clone back some of the color from the Clone Source, I suggest the **Opaque Round Impasto** brush, with Clone Color enabled (click the rubber stamp icon in the Colors palette).

Smear Me Twice...

Notice that the **Resat** (resaturation) value for **Smeary Varnish** is zero, indicating that no new color will be applied. Play a bit with this brush to get the feel of it, and consider tweaking its behavior by adjusting one or more variables in the Property Bar. Figure 5.12 shows a practice area with Smeary Varnish strokes.

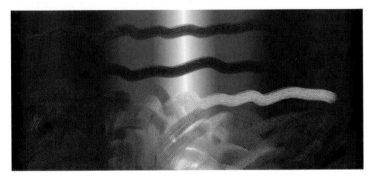

Figure 5.12

Smear me twice...

Figure 5.13

In-depth analysis.

Another variable that influences the look of an Impasto stroke is the amount of depth. This control is not available on the Property Bar but is found in the Brush Controls palette via the Window menu. Figure 5.13 shows the Impasto control panel. Notice the default Depth setting for **Smeary Varnish** is 12%. See what happens when you change that amount.

Apply some Smeary Varnish to the background, using longer strokes in several directions. Figure 5.14 is a detail showing the variety of textures and colors created by Impasto brushes along with the Coarse Oily strokes. Strive for variety in the amount of detail as well. Some areas should be smoother and simpler to give the eyes a place to rest. The finished painting of Audrey appears in Figure 5.15. Now it's time to soak those brushes in turpentine— oh, never mind!

Figure 5.14
Varied brushstrokes.

Figure 5.15
Audrey in oils.

Painting Backward

I often take digital paintings and project them onto real canvas in order to create alternative versions in traditional media. This time we'll use an oil painting made from a photo and reverse engineer it for a digital version. I've never done this before, but it seems to me inspiration can flow in any direction. If it doesn't work out, no harm done.

Figure 5.16 is a photo of my artist friend Miles standing near the window of my Sausalito painting studio. I like this simple pose with strong directional lighting, as well as the absence of a smile. I generally ask people I photograph not to smile…most have a hard time overcoming that annoying habit. If we're going to imitate traditional painting, it's unlikely that your model will be smiling for the 8 or 12 hours necessary for the sitting (or standing).

Figure 5.16
Miles standing.

Figure 5.17 shows my traditional oil painting based on this photo, part of my "Men with Beards" series. It was painted on a 24×30-inch canvas and took a few weeks, what with having to wait for parts to dry before I could work on it some more. Earlier stages in the development of this painting are shown in Figure 5.18. These images are all available in the Lesson 5 folder on the book's CD. The JPEG files are named Miles_oil1 through 4, and I suggest you open them now. You'll use them as guides for creating a digital portrait, but allow your work to go in other directions if it needs to. At least we won't have to wait for it to dry!

Figure 5.17
Man with beard.

Figure 5.18
Miles to go.

Be Prepared

Start by selecting **File > Clone** to make a copy of the Miles photo. Don't use Quick Clone because you don't want the copy deleted. You'll be working directly on the copy. Save the copy in RIFF format so you can use **Iterative Save** as you work. Be sure to leave the original photo open to function as a Clone Source when you need it.

Open the **Underpainting** palette and apply the **Sketchbook** color scheme. Move the **Hue** and **Saturation** sliders to the left for the result shown in Figure 5.19, a dull purplish monochrome with a flattened tonal range.

Figure 5.19

Miles dull and flat.

Make a Mess

We still need to eliminate most of the details. Use the **Water Rake** from the **Blender** category to make juicy, brushy smears all over the image. Use shorter strokes when working on the face, and bigger energetic strokes on the shirt and background. Follow the contours of shapes as you work. Yes, these techniques are similar to those used in the painting of Audrey. Figure 5.20 is a close approximation to the first stage in my traditional painting. It actually works as a reasonably successful piece already, if you like a loose gestural style, and I do. Make sure you save this stage.

Figure 5.20
Looking rakish.

The Range and the Planes

Make a new layer for the next stage and import another custom palette into your workspace. It's called Colormix brushes, and you'll see very soon why that name is appropriate. Choose **Thick Gouache Round 30** from the custom palette. Real life gouache (rhymes with "gosh") is water-based but opaque and will serve for building up the painting at this stage. This variant has a subtle amount of depth that's just right. We're not going for strong Impasto effects this time.

Bring stage 2 of the oil painting (Miles_oil2.jpg) to the front of your stack of open images and choose **New Color Set from Image** in the **Color Sets** popup menu. This will provide all the blueish purples, lavenders, and peachy flesh tones needed for now. Use this image and the enhanced photo (refer to Figure 5.19) as references to block in the darkest areas with deep blues and purples. You'll be establishing a fuller range of values. The strong light source from the upper right will help determine where highlights and shadows belong. It's useful to think of shapes and planes as you establish the structure of the painting. Work with large size brushes to keep from getting too picky. I suggest the **Real Stubby Blender** for smearing and smoothing. Because you are work-ing on a layer, you'll need to check the **Pick Up Underlying Color** option on the Layers palette. Figure 5.21 is a reasonable facsimile of the oil painting at this point.

Figure 5.21
By golly, by gouache!

Mix and Match

In a traditional studio, you'd have a slab of wood or glass for mixing paint with a palette knife to get the colors you want. Welcome to Painter's digital **Mixer** palette, nestled between the standard Colors palette and Color Sets, unless you moved it. Figure 5.22 shows the Mixer with its popup menu open. It's worth taking a few minutes to get acquainted with the amazing capabilities of this palette.

To get colors onto the pad, choose from the tiny swatches at the top and use the **Apply Color** tool, whose icon is a paintbrush. Mix colors with the palette knife—just like real life. If **Dirty Brush** mode is enabled, the mixing brush will begin with the current color and blend it with the colors on the pad. To pick your main color for painting, click inside the pad with the familiar **Sample Color** dropper. The **Sample Multiple Colors** tool is a dropper on steroids! Click it where two or more colors meet or blend. It won't change the main color in the Colors palette, but it will enable you to paint multicolor strokes with certain brushes. That's why I named the custom palette shown in Figure 5.23 Colormix Brushes. All of them are capable of being loaded with multiple colors. They include the following categories (from left to right): Artists' Oils, Gouache, Impasto, Acrylics, Oils, Watercolor, and RealBristle Brushes.

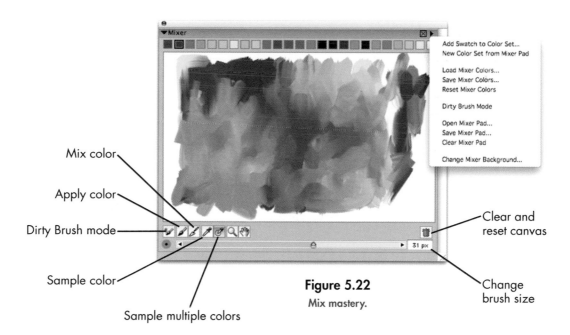

Mix color

Apply color

Dirty Brush mode

Sample color

Sample multiple colors

Clear and reset canvas

Change brush size

Figure 5.22

Mix mastery.

Figure 5.23

Multicolor brushes.

I used the Sample Multiple Colors tool to click near the right edge of the Mixer pad where red, purple, and teal blue meet to get the brush strokes shown in Figure 5.24. Clear the Mixer pad by clicking its trashcan.

Figure 5.24

Multicolor strokes.

Complementary, My Dear Watson!

I used a lot of purple for the preliminary stages, then finished with a complementary palette (colors opposite each other on the color wheel), mostly blues and oranges. A range of blue and orange hues blended in various proportions and in a variety of saturations and values will provide all the colors needed for this painting. Each of the little swatches in the Mixer pad can be filled with the current main color by holding the Cmd/Ctrl key as you click in the swatch you want to change. Use any method you like to get a few blues and orange swatches into the Mixer. Include a yellow-orange for flesh tones and a purple or two for the underpainting. Black and white will be useful to make shades and tints.

Batches of Swatches

The Mixer and Color Sets palettes make a powerful combination. A great way to find colors for the Mixer is to make a Color Set from the Miles painting, then choose your swatches from that set. Later, you can make a new Color Set from the mixture you made on the Mixer pad. The popup menu on the Mixer lets you save what's on the pad, as well as the swatches. No need to worry about running out of a special flesh tone—as long as a single pixel exists somewhere, you can make more.

Show Us Your Swatches

Painter 11 introduces expandable color palettes, which are especially useful when you want lots of Mixer space and more than a few color swatches. Just move the Mixer away from its palette group and drag the lower-right corner to resize it.

Consider the Source

Use the final stage of the oil painting (Miles_oil4.jpg) for visual guidance from this point on. Even more importantly, if you want to achieve a reasonable likeness of Miles, look again and again at his actual face! For an ideal reference image, Painter offers a terrific way to combine the accuracy of the photo with the colors of my painting.

With the original photo of Miles as the active image, select **Effects > Tonal Control > Match Palette**. Choose the finished oil painting in the **Source** field and drag the **Color** and **Brightness** sliders to the maximum. Figure 5.25 shows my settings, and Figure 5.26 has a detail of the results.

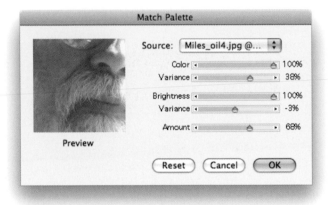

Figure 5.25

Got a match?

Figure 5.26

Color to the max.

final Arrangements

With your working canvas enlarged and two other reference images open, you'll need to organize the remaining screen real estate as efficiently as possible. It will help to have your Color Set and Mixer open near each other and most other palettes closed and out of the way. Save the configuration by selecting **Window > Arrange Palettes > Save Layout**.

More Face Time

To refine your Color Set for working on the head, make a Lasso or Oval selection of Miles' head in the oil painting and choose **New Color Set from Selection** in the **Color Sets** popup menu. Choose a larger Swatch Size for convenience.

Zoom in 150% or better on the current version of your digital painting. Instead of making another layer for developing the face and head, continue painting on top of what you have. You probably don't need a safety net anymore, but if things go terribly wrong you can always establish an earlier version as the clone source.

Time to choose brush variants for this stage. Emulating traditional techniques, we will work with thicker paint now using the "fat over lean" rule. Let's explore some candidates, using a new blank canvas for "scratch" and some test strokes on our working image. I like the way **Dry Clumpy Impasto** from the **Artists' Oils** category works on the beard, especially when blended with strokes from **Thick Wet Camel 20**, an Oils variant. Figure 5.27 shows how they can work in tandem. To make Thick Wet Camel a smeary brush with no added color, just reduce its default Resat value of 8% to zero. Save this new variant as **Thick Camel Smeary**. It will be handy to have around permanently. Clumpy Impasto is not an Italian appetizer but one of those colormixer variants, so take full advantage of it by using your Mixer pad and the Sample Multiple Colors tool. The practice strokes in Figure 5.28 were made using the Mixer pad I created from color swatches taken from the new Color Set (refer to Figure 5.22).

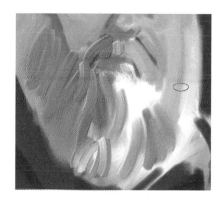

Figure 5.27
Dry and clumpy, thick and wet.

Figure 5.28
Pass the Impasto, please.

Vary Similitude

You'll want to vary the size of the Dry Clumpy Impasto brush as you work, for verisimilitude ("truthiness"). The 74% Depth setting can also be changed in the Impasto control panel (refer to Figure 5.13). Another variable of interest is **Viscosity**, available in the Property Bar. I didn't notice it when I was making short strokes in the beard, but this brush runs out of paint, depending on the amount of viscosity. Increase viscosity to run out of color sooner. Yes, thicker is quicker.

Slightly smoother brush effects are desirable for the flesh areas, and some multicolor strokes will be useful here, too. The **Wet Brush** variant of Artists' Oils will do nicely. It is very similar to Dry Clumpy Impasto, but it does not have a depth component. Our new variant, Thick Camel Smeary, can be applied here and there to give a bit of Impasto "body" to Wet Brush strokes on the skin. As for areas where you'd like to eliminate some thickness, use the **Depth Equalizer** from the **Impasto** category.

Thick on the Draw

Open the Impasto control panel and observe the Draw To field as you switch between variants. A Draw To setting of Color and Depth results in thick paint, while the Color setting creates flat paint. What do you suppose happens when you select only Depth as a Draw To setting?

Best for Last

We're in the home stretch now. Have you been putting your brush variants into a custom palette for this project as you go? Well, it's not too late. You'll be swapping among five or six variants, so a custom palette will make life much easier. Create your own or import Miles Brushes from the Palettes and Libraries folder on the CD that accompanies this book. I've organized the palette shown in Figure 5.29 according to the stages in the painting. Each stage has involved using more brushes.

The default Wet Brush is 20 pixels, and I made a smaller one that I saved and dragged into the custom palette so I wouldn't have to keep fiddling with size controls. The Detail Oils 15 brush will be needed for details (obviously) that just can't be handled by the Wet Brush variants. Figure 5.30 shows how far I was able to get before relying on the small Detail Oils for finishing touches.

You can decide how you want to handle finishing the painting of the shirt and the background. Something similar to the traditional painting can be achieved with large brushes. Experiment using some variants you haven't tried yet. Keep it visually simple so the focus remains on Miles' head.

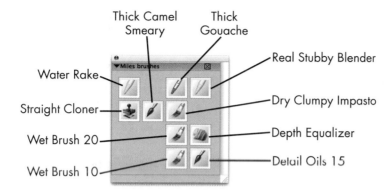

Figure 5.29
Customize me.

Figure 5.30
Quit when you're a head.

What's Next?

Congratulations on completing the basic lessons in digital painting! In the chapters to follow, you'll find advanced projects, and you'll be invited to play with some exciting Painter features that go way beyond simply imitating natural media.

You may already have some favorite Painter tools and a preference for certain subjects to draw and paint. Are you also developing a style of your own? I encourage you to be open to working in a variety of styles, choosing among them when you begin a new project. Painter makes it so easy to switch from pencil sketching to oil painting to chalk drawing. Don't be surprised if I ask you to combine all of those techniques, and more, in one project.

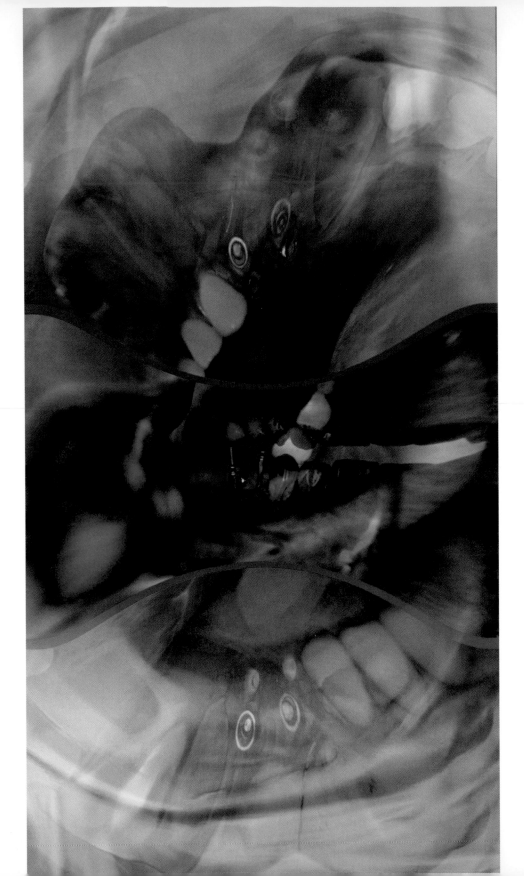

PART

II

Beyond the Basics

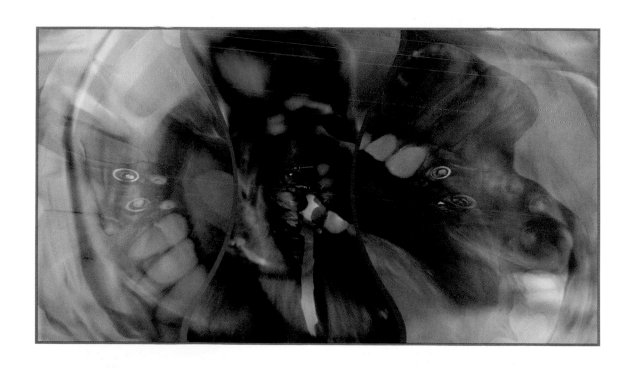

6 Graphics Techniques

Are you ready to work with some of the more advanced tools and features of Painter? I'll just assume you responded "yes" and continue. The projects in this lesson are not more difficult than those in the first section of the book. In fact, for those of you still developing your freehand sketching skills and eye-hand coordination, these projects might be a bit easier than earlier assignments. That's because you will rely on some digital tricks that don't necessarily depend on your drawing and painting skills. You'll still need to make creative decisions, though, and there will be plenty of them.

Graphic Language

The term *graphic* can refer to an illustration or design composed of simple shapes and flat color fills. The word might be used to describe any bold or hard-edged style, regardless of media, as well as a commercial-looking piece of artwork. Another reference is *fine art prints*, such as silkscreen or relief prints. All those definitions will be useful in this lesson.

It's Only a Mask

In traditional printmaking and airbrush painting, areas can be protected from paint or ink with a mask. These can be made from tape or cardboard or self-adhesive frisket paper cut to the precise shape needed. It shouldn't surprise you that in digital art, creating masks is much easier.

Pixel-based applications like Painter and Photoshop provide several tools for selecting portions of the canvas to accept painted strokes or effects. Whatever isn't selected is, by definition, masked. You can make selections based on geometric shapes, or draw freehand selections around an irregular area using the **Lasso** tool. Painter 11 introduces the **Polygon Lasso** tool for selecting shapes with straight edges. A sophisticated selection tool that has no counterpart in traditional media is the **Magic Wand**, which selects all pixels in a defined color range. Figure 6.1 shows where the Selection tools are located on the Toolbox. Notice the **Selection Adjuster** tool, which allows you to move or resize a selection marquee. The Property Bar shows that the Oval Selection tool is currently active. Choices are available for adding to or subtracting from a selection using any of the selection tools. This allows you to create some very fancy selection areas. The bottom-left corner of any image you're working with has options for painting inside or outside the selection or ignoring the selection altogether.

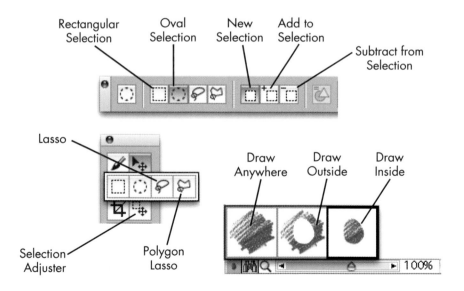

Figure 6.1

Selection, selection, selection.

When the Ants Come Marching In

An active selection (of whatever shape) has a moving marquee that looks like an animated dashed line. The cute nickname for this is *marching ants*. You might want to turn off the marching ants (without losing the selection) to see your work better. The **Hide Marquee** command in the **Select** menu has a keyboard shortcut: **Shift,Cmd/Ctrl+H**.

Once you make a selection, you can paint it without the need to be careful at the edges. You can also use the **Paint Bucket** tool to fill a selection instantly with your choice from the Property Bar: current color, gradient, pattern, or weave. An especially dandy command in the **Select** menu is **Stroke Selection.** This will automatically paint the edges of your selection with the current color, using the current brush variant.

A Masked Ball

The Select menu offers commands for altering and managing selections. There is also a special **Library** palette, the **Selection Portfolio**, with a collection of common (and not so common) selections you can simply drag to the canvas. Let's play with selections on a new canvas about 850 pixels wide by 500 pixels high. Open the **Selection Portfolio** and load the **Spiral** selections from the **Extras** folder in the **Painter X or 11** application folder, then drag the **Rough Spiral** to your canvas. If you're using an earlier version of Painter, choose the spiral from the default portfolio shown in Figure 6.2.

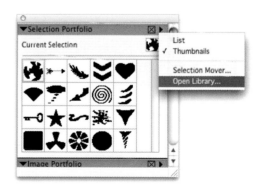

Figure 6.2
Just drag and drop.

Fancy-Schmancy

Figure 6.3 has a sampling of creative ways to work with a selection. Each time I dragged in a new Spiral selection, I resized or rotated it with either the Selection Adjuster tool or (new in Painter 11) the Transform tool. Here are the techniques I used (top row from left to right, then bottom row). Feel free to use other combinations. This will give you an opportunity to poke around in some of Painter's special effects tools.

- Fill with current color (pink), then Stroke Selection with Impasto > Acid Etch brush.

- Choose Select > Invert (this makes the selection a mask, so it is protected), then paint freely with an Artists' Oils variant and multiple colors picked up from the Mixer pad.

- Choose Lotus Petals from the Pattern library, then Stroke Selection with Pattern Pen Masked. (The Pattern Pen category will be discussed shortly.)

- Fill with the current pattern (Lotus Petals), then stroke with the Real Fine Point Pen in black.

- Fill with a gradient (Sea Foam). Choose Select > Float Selection to place the item on a new layer, then apply Effects > Objects > Create Drop Shadow.

- Fill with golden yellow. For the 3-D effect, choose Bevel World from the Dynamic plug-ins found at the bottom of the Layers palette.

Figure 6.3
Stroke and fill and. . .

Image Outsourcing

To fill a selection with a pattern, you must choose Source Image from the Property Bar. Confused? Read on. When you want to establish a source image for Cloner brushes, the **File > Clone Source** list includes **Current Pattern** as a choice. This may be less confusing if you simply think of the current pattern as the default Clone Source. What do you think will happen if you have an open image as the designated Clone Source and you use Source Image to fill a selection? The answer is revealed in Figure 6.4. I made a complex selection using the Oval Selection tool several times with the Add to Selection option enabled in the Property Bar (the Shift key also works as an Add To function). With aquarium1.jpg from the Nature folder opened, I checked it in the File > Clone Source list. I used the Paint Bucket tool to fill with the source image, and sure enough, I got the underwater scene inside the bubble-shaped selection. Finally, I floated the selection and added the drop-shadow effect.

Figure 6.4
Fish in a bubble.

Masked and Unmasked

Let's explore the amazing **Pattern Pen** category. Take a look at the strokes in Figure 6.5. Most of these strokes were made with the **Pattern Pen Masked** variant. The difference between the masked and the "not masked" variant is demonstrated with the two **Double Helix** strokes. The blue background that is part of the Double Helix pattern is masked out when you use Pattern Pen Masked. When I scribble with the masked Double Helix, I think of it as my linguine brush! In the lower right of the figure, **Wave Mosaic** is also painted both masked and—the other way. ("Unmasked" can't be the right word for a stroke that includes a strip of background color. It makes me think of somebody being forced to reveal his true identity.) The potential for decorative, expressive, and whimsical uses of Pattern Pens will be explored in other lessons.

Figure 6.5
Strokes of genius.

Can't find the Snakes or the Blonde Braid?

I gathered my favorite patterns from several versions of Painter into one library. It's called **Rhoda Patterns** and is available in the **Pals & Libs** folder on the CD that came with this book. Just use the **Open Library** command in the **Pattern** pop-up menu. You can easily reshuffle patterns from several libraries by using the **Pattern Mover** utility. The same kind of function is provided for papers, gradients, and so on. See "Organize Your Papers" in Lesson 3 for step-by-step instructions on using a Mover.

Airless Brushes

The ideal brush category for working with selection masks is **Airbrushes**. Traditional airbrushes spray tiny droplets of pigment mixed with compressed air. The instrument connected to that compressed air source is a metal device with a nozzle and a small reservoir for pigment. It has a couple of tiny wheels for finger control of the size of the spray and the density and coarseness of the droplets. It takes quite a bit of practice to get skilled with a traditional airbrush. Painter lets you shave months, even years, off that process.

Graffiti

Make a new canvas for trying out several of the Airbrush variants. Figure 6.6 shows some airbrush practice. The variants used here include Broad Wheel, Coarse Spray, Variable Splatter, Tiny Spattery, and Fine Tip Soft Air. Make an Airbrush sampler of your own. Check out the realistic response to the tilt and bearing of your Wacom pen as you change its angle and direction. Notice what happens when you pause a bit during an airbrush stroke: Pigment keeps on spraying! Use some of the Selection Portfolio items to experiment with. Try spraying both inside and outside a selection with different colors. The worm shape and the spiral arrow show a basic technique for creating the illusion of depth: Spray a slightly darker color for the shadow side and slightly lighter for the highlights. Remember to be consistent with your imaginary light source.

Figure 6.6
Fresh air.

All the Angles

For a visual cue to the tilt of your pen, turn on Enhanced Brush Ghosting in Painter Preferences.

Airless Landscape

The imaginary landscape in Figure 6.7 can be created with a combination of smooth and coarse Airbrush variants and selection masks made with the Lasso and Polygon Lasso tools. You will want to save your masks for repeated use. The RIFF files showing the development of this piece in the Lessons folder on the CD include the saved selections.

These are the Airbrush variants I suggest for different parts of the artwork:

- **Soft Airbrush (various sizes):** Mountains, hills, tulips

- **Pepper Spray:** Cloud, sky, green highlights

- **Coarse Spray:** Snow on mountain tops

- **Variable Splatter:** Wildflowers

- **Broad Wheel Airbrush:** Foreground grasses

- **Tiny Spattery Airbrush:** Forest behind hills

Re-create this whimsical landscape with me. Start with a white canvas 1500 pixels wide by 1200 pixels high. Make a Lasso selection similar to the one shown in Figure 6.8, and spray two shades of blue above it for the sky.

Figure 6.7
A happy place.

Quick Invert

You'll need to invert selections frequently to paint outside of them, then toggle back to the original selection. The easiest way to do this is with the keyboard shortcut **Cmd/Ctrl+I**.

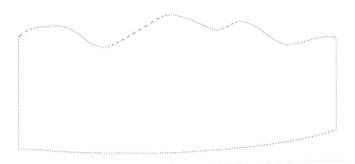

Figure 6.8

Ants march over mountains.

Save the selection, naming it Mountains. When you use the Save Selection command, a new channel is created. Open the **Channels** palette and keep it handy for the rest of this project. You can see each of your saved selections as a black-and-white mask and find icons for saving, loading, and inverting them. Those options are also available in the Select menu. Figure 6.9 shows my Channels palette after the next step, painting a cloud.

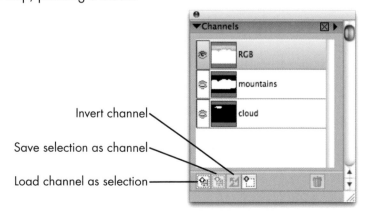

Figure 6.9

Tune in your channels.

Seeing Red

If you turn on the visibility (eyeball icon) of a channel, it will show up in your image as a transparent red area. This is a tribute to the historical fact that traditional masking film was red in color.

Make a fluffy cloud shape with the Lasso tool and paint it as shown in Figure 6.10, using a darker blue for the underside. Save this selection and all the selections you make for this painting.

Figure 6.10
Partly cloudy.

You need the Mountains selection again, so load it with either the **Load Selection** command or by clicking the corresponding icon at the bottom of the Channels palette. The Load Selection dialog appears, as shown in Figure 6.11. Choose Mountains from the list and accept the default Operation setting Replace Selection. Notice that the other possibilities include adding to or subtracting from a selection. They will be useful a bit later.

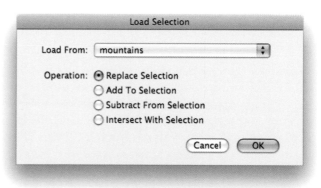

Figure 6.11
Loading a selection.

For a soft edge, choose **Select > Feather** to apply a 12-pixel blur, then spray a light purple color for the upper mountain range. Make a second mountain range with the Lasso tool or use the Selection Adjuster tool to maneuver the original mountain selection into a lower position. I reduced the Feather amount to zero, and for variety I flipped it horizontally. There doesn't seem to be a way to do this automatically, so I dragged one edge across to the opposite side, then pulled the second edge out the other way. Kids, don't try this at home . . . and don't confuse this transformation with the **Invert** command, which deselects all selected areas and vice versa. Use a slightly darker purple for this section. The results at this point are shown in Figure 6.12. The irregular application of color implies some mist and shadows in the mountains. Imperfections can result in "happy accidents."

Figure 6.12
Purple mountains majesty.

Make a new **Lasso** selection for the green hills and fill it with a solid coat of green using a **Soft** or **Broad** variant. Add some lighter green highlights with **Pepper Spray**. Figure 6.13 shows the bottom half of the landscape with additional elements. The suggestion of tree tops behind the hills (refer to Figure 6.7) was created with irregular strokes of the **Tiny Spattery Airbrush**. This brush has built-in variations in hue, saturation, and value (as you can see from the **Color Variability** palette), so the illusion of depth is enhanced.

Figure 6.13
The hills are alive.

The spiky grass was created with a **Polygon Lasso** selection, saved and flipped for the second application of a darker green. The wildflowers behind the grass are the result of three quick strokes (each in a different color) with the **Variable Splatter** brush.

For the final version, snow has been sprinkled on the distant mountains with a few touches of the **Coarse Spray**. Remember to feather the Mountains selection again after you load it. The tulips in the foreground are a set of three shapes made with the **Lasso** tool, using the **Add to Selection** feature. They were saved as a single selection and loaded several times, then moved and resized as needed. Tulip shadows are made with a 20-pixel soft airbrush, and the delicate stems were painted with **Fine Detail Air 8**.

Notice the shadow on the distant mountains made by the cloud? This required loading the original Mountains selection, then loading the reversed mountains using the **Subtract from Selection** operation so the other mountain range could be protected when the shadow was painted in.

So, it turns out that airbrush art doesn't have to be slick, smooth, and realistic. And it doesn't necessarily have to feature either sports cars or what used to be called "pinup" girls.

Fine Art Printmaking

Painter offers several ways to imitate printmaking techniques, such as silkscreens, woodcuts, and lithographs. A woodcut, or wood block print, is a labor-intensive technique that involves making several "plates," each carved into the surface of the wood to generate a portion of the final image. Every plate must be inked by hand and carefully lined up, or *registered*, so that it is in the proper position for pressure to be applied manually or with a special press. The procedure is time-consuming, painstaking, and messy—did I mention you have to use sharp tools and could easily hurt yourself?

What a Relief!

You'll stay clean and relatively safe using Painter's **Woodcut** effect. Incidentally, woodcuts are considered relief prints because ink is applied to the uncut surface, while the incised lines and carved out areas of the block leave the paper unmarked. A good candidate for the woodcut look is an image with strong line definition or bold textures. Let's work with fish_skeleton.jpg, shown in Figure 6.14, a specimen I photographed at the California Academy of Sciences in San Francisco.

Figure 6.14

Dem bones.

Clean up the photo to minimize or eliminate background elements, such as the structure the fish is mounted on. First, we'll clone fish pixels over the dark vertical bar hiding part of the tail. Choose the **Rubber Stamp**, sharing a space in the Toolbox with the Cloner brush. Press the **Option/Alt** key and click the point shown in Figure 6.15, indicated by the green dot with the number 1. This establishes the source pixel for point-to-point cloning. Release the modifier key and paint a few vertical strokes on the dark bar. You've repaired the fish tail seamlessly!

The remaining background can quickly be neutralized with a series of Magic Wand selections (use the **Add to Selection** option) filled with light gray. Paint out any stray areas with the same gray. A few rough edges are fine for our purposes.

Choose **Effects > Surface Control > Woodcut** and notice the array of settings available. Figure 6.16 displays the Woodcut dialog box, showing that settings for **Output Black** and **Output Color** are separate (and you can turn off either one). We'll take advantage of the independence of black from color in our preparation, so cancel the effect for now. Make a copy of the image (**Select > All**, then **Edit > Copy**) and use **Edit > Paste** to automatically create a new layer with the identical image. Now you can apply color effects to the canvas and black to the layer copy.

Turn off visibility of the layer copy, and target (highlight) the canvas. Open the **Woodcut** effect again.

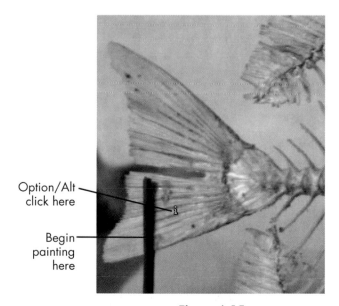

Option/Alt
click here

Begin
painting
here

Figure 6.15
Clean the fish.

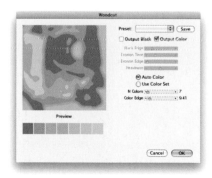

Figure 6.16
Fish head.

Effects Access

The last effect you invoked (even if you cancelled it) will be at the top of the Effects menu, so it's easy to find again. It's even easier if you access it with the keyboard shortcut **Cmd/Ctrl + /** (forward slash).

Disable **Output Black** and move the color sliders around until you like what you see in the Preview window. Traditional woodcuts tend to have a limited number of colors, so I reduced the **N Colors** to 7. Move the slider for **Color Edge** to the right until you like the degree of simplification of color shapes. You can enable Output Black and fiddle with those controls to envision the final effects, but turn it off again before you click OK. The **Output Color** layer is shown in Figure 6.17 on the left. I accepted the default **Auto Color** setting, but imagine the fun you can have with an alternate Color Set.

Time to switch our attention to the layer copy. Make it visible and highlight it. Call up the Woodcut effect again. Use Output Black this time and your judgment about what settings produce a pleasing amount of black detail.

 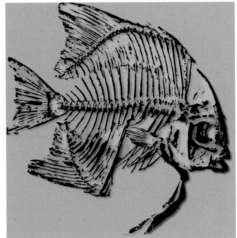

Figure 6.17
Blackened fish.

Click OK, and you'll get a black-and-white result. Do you recall how to make the white parts of a layer transparent so the canvas colors can show through? If you said the **Gel** or **Multiply** composite method, you're absolutely right! But check out **Soft Light**, too. It's more subtle, and that's not always a bad thing.

So, one reason to have the effect on two separate layers is to play with composite methods. Here's another: You can create the effect of imperfect alignment by shifting the layer a few pixels to right or left and up or down. The right half of Figure 6.17 shows the finished woodcut, with the layers just enough out of register to give the illusion that this is a fine art print made the hard way.

Faux Silkscreen

A silkscreen print, or *serigraph*, is created by squeezing ink through a fine mesh onto paper or t-shirts, fabric, whatever. An image is created because parts of the mesh screen are protected from the ink with some kind of resistant fluid, or "resist." As with relief prints, several passes can be made using different screen designs and different colors. Photographic images can be transformed into silkscreen graphics, and these are most successful when the original images are simplified.

Well, Painter has a **Serigraphy** effect in the **Surface Control** group, right near the Woodcut effect. But we're not gonna use it. We can get better control and more exciting options using another combination of effects to imitate a silkscreen print. Let's use another image from the bone collection. The skull of a warthog is shown in Figure 6.18. No need to clean up the background, except maybe for the lettering on the card.

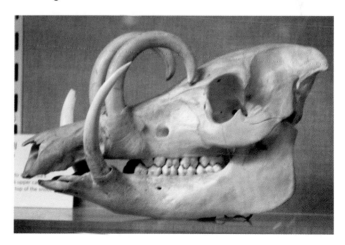

Figure 6.18

Horny devil.

Make a copy of the skull on another layer, as you did for the Woodcut exercise. We'll use **Effects > Surface Control > Apply Screen** on the new layer. (It's okay if you start with the canvas image.) The **Apply Screen** dialog, shown in Figure 6.19, allows you to reduce the full range of tonality to just three flat colors—any three colors you want. You also get to determine the threshold for both color changes. Click on a swatch to pick a color, then experiment with both Threshold sliders. Be sure to switch to **Image Luminance** in the **Using** field. My results show some accidental-looking bits of color in the background. These are great— don't even think about eliminating them.

Your darkest color swatch should be on the left and the lightest on the right if you want to map the original value range. For a negative effect, reverse that order. For some wild solarization, have lightest (or darkest) color in the middle. Sound familiar? You worked with value maps in Chapter 5, when you applied gradient colors to an image.

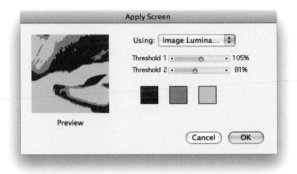

Figure 6.19

Lipstick on a pig.

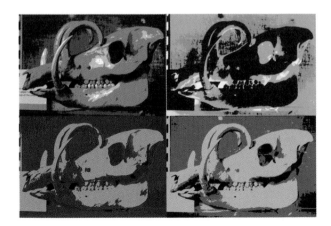

Figure 6.20

Andy Warthog.

This is already a bold graphic, but we still have another layer to play with. Apply **Effects > Tonal Control > Posterize** with four levels. Or load a wild color set (Purplish Coppers works nicely) and use **Tonal Control > Posterize Using Color Set.** Now comes the fun of exploring different composite methods. You might like several combinations, so be sure to save each one. Figure 6.20 displays a grid of color variations, hinting at the pop art screen prints of the sixties.

Liquid Ink

The **Liquid Ink** brushes can yield exciting results even if you aren't completely sure how they work. Your beginner's mind may come into play in this section. Some of the effects you can achieve resemble *encaustic*, a method for painting with layers of hot wax. The last time I painted anything with hot wax, painful ripping of unwanted hair was involved. So, we won't do anything like that.

Wet and Sticky

Some Liquid Ink strokes tend to stick to each other, a quality that can be seen in Figure 6.21 where circular strokes that were made with the **Smooth Camel** variant touch each other. Other Liquid Ink brushes can create rough edges and crumbling textures. Let's examine some of the special features of this category. Open the **Brush Creator** and click on the **Stroke Designer** section, shown in Figure 6.22.

Figure 6.21
Sticky circles.

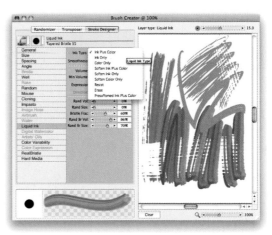

Figure 6.22
Brush tester.

Even if you don't want to customize a brush variant, the Stroke Designer is an ideal place to scribble and get acquainted with all the variables that define brush behavior in one compact space. A Brush Selector Bar is included, as are the Brush Controls, a stroke thumbnail, and a scratch pad.

There are close to 60 variants in the Liquid Ink category, but the much shorter Ink Type list (similar to the Dab type for other categories) suggests the basic kinds of behavior you can get. The purple and red squiggles at the top of Figure 6.23 were painted with two strokes of the **Tapered Thick Bristle** variant using its default type, **Ink Plus Color**. Changing the type to **Ink Only** results in a black stroke, regardless of your current color. A switch to **Color Only** means you can only see your stroke on top of existing ink, as the gold color painted across the black shows. I had an inkling (sorry!) the gold would show up if I scribbled more Ink Only over it (under it?), and that's exactly what happened. The bottom sample shows a blend between colors made when **Soften Color Only** is brushed over the original two strokes.

Figure 6.23
Some ink types.

Reverting to Type

Instead of searching through the 50-plus variants to find the ones that already had the Ink Types I wanted to test, I just switched Ink Type for the Tapered Thick Bristle. Not a bad way to work, if you remember to use the Restore Default Variant command in the Brush Selector menu after you're done.

Resist reacts as you'd expect if you work with traditional screen prints or lithography. Ink is repelled, as shown in the left half of Figure 6.24. What you might not expect is the capacity of **Resist** brushes to scrape ink away after it's been applied, as in the right half. The only difference between these two examples is that I couldn't see the stroke I made on the left until I painted over it with an **Ink Plus Color** variant.

You can add 3D thickness to existing Liquid Ink strokes and actually change the width of brushstrokes after they have been applied. Double-click a **Liquid Ink** layer in the **Layers** palette to access the special **Layer Attributes** dialog, shown in Figure 6.25. The Amount slider changes 3D height (similar to Impasto depth), and Threshold changes how much of the edges of a stroke are revealed. Use the handy Notes section to jot down the names of variants used, or any ideas you may have for working the image, or a grocery list.

Figure 6.24

Resistance is fertile.

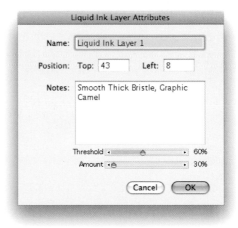

Figure 6.25

Layer attributes.

The top of Figure 6.26 shows strokes made with **Smooth Thick Bristle** and **Graphic Camel**. (I know that because I wrote it down in the Notes section of Layer Attributes.) The bottom shows the Amount (height) of the Smooth Thick Bristle stroke increased from zero to 40%. The Graphic Camel stroke shows the Threshold increased to about 110%, looking similar to a Resist effect. These changes are nondestructive, meaning you can change these values over and over without reducing the quality of the image.

Figure 6.26
Amount and threshold.

Fish Redux

I hope you like fish, 'cause we're having it again. Open either the original fish_skeleton.jpg or the retouched version. Make a Quick Clone so you can use it for tracing. Choose a grayish yellow color and paint a rough background with the **Sparse Camel** variant. Figure 6.27 shows the image with tracing paper at 70%.

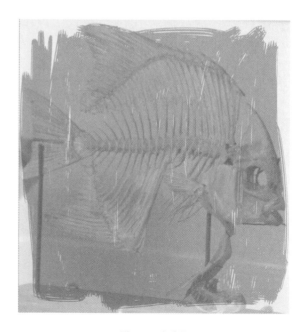

Figure 6.27
Sparsely painted.

Make a new Liquid Ink layer and sketch the fish in dark brown with the **Fine Point** variant. Add some height to the brush strokes on the first Liquid Ink layer by increasing the Amount slider to 10%. Figure 6.28 shows the image at this stage.

Figure 6.28
Heightened fish with sparsely.

Add another Liquid Ink layer and switch back to the Sparse Camel for a fatter fish sketch. I used a warm pinkish color—okay, salmon. The left side of Figure 6.29 shows this version with the Fine Point layer hidden. Let's scrape away some of this layer. Raising the Threshold setting would work, but I want to have more control, so I used the Sparse Camel Resist brush. The results are seen on the right in Figure 6.29.

Figure 6.29

Scraped salmon.

Height was added to the salmon layer by raising the Amount slider to 20%. I wanted to push the primitive look of the piece, so I duplicated the Fine Point sketch layer and painted strokes over parts of it with the **Soften Edges** variant, resulting in seemingly random blobs of ink. That layer is shown alone in Figure 6.30.

Figure 6.30

Blotted fish.

Duplicity

Duplicate any layer with the **Layer Adjuster** tool active and holding down the **Option/Alt** key as you double-click on that layer in the image.

Finally, I changed my Sparse Camel brush to Color Only so I could replace the original background with something a bit more interesting. Edges of the new colors were softened, and bits of the previous background were allowed to show through. I switched the composite method of the original Fine Point sketch to Overlay, getting some unexpected red lines here and there. The final state is seen in Figure 6.31. Not sure if it's really finished. You can keep developing it, using the stages provided in the Lesson 6 folder on the book's CD.

Figure 6.31
Blue-green plate special.

What's Next?

The advanced features you played with in this lesson are worthy of a lot more investigation, and you are cordially invited to explore them more fully with or without my directions. In lessons yet to come, you'll have an opportunity to combine and hone your skills while you delve into even more exciting and exotic brushes, features, and effects.

7 Mixed~Up Media

Mixed media was mentioned way back in Lesson 2. It refers to artwork that combines two or more techniques that are traditionally separate. Even putting pencil strokes on a painting qualifies. Imagine the excitement early in the 20th century when *avant garde* artists were pasting photos, newspaper clippings, and small objects on their canvasses! Painter takes the mixing of media to a whole 'nuther level. You painted with patterns in Lesson 6—by the time you finish this lesson, you will know how to paint with liquid metal, melted chocolate, barbed wire, flowers, and (yuk!) insects.

Way Out Graphics

There are several brush categories and variants that allow you to go way past mixing media and into the realm of special effects. Figure 7.1 has a sampling of strokes you're invited to try, and there is a custom palette in the **Pals & Libs** folder on the CD to give you some encouragement. It's called **Special Effects** and is shown in Figure 7.2.

Figure 7.1
Wild, weird stuff.

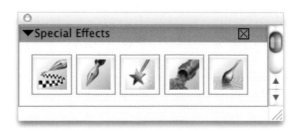

Figure 7.2
Special F-X starter kit.

If that stroke on the far left in Figure 7.1 seems familiar, then you haven't forgotten **Pattern Pen Masked.** The pattern used here is called **Vivid Seed Pods**. Moving to the right, you see a stroke made with a Pens variant, but this one doesn't use the current color—it paints with the current gradient! Gradient pens come in two flavors, and both are shown here. **Grad Pen** uses all the colors in a gradient and squeezes them down the stroke like toothpaste. **Grad Repeat Pen** performs as advertised, repeating all the colors in strips that run perpendicular to the stroke. I don't think they can do that with toothpaste—yet.

The next two strokes, named **Piano Keys** and **Furry Brush**, are members of the **F-X** category, which has a Magic Wand icon. The spray of gardenias, string of candy, and stack of sushi slices were all made by the amazing **Image Hose**. In order to demonstrate some distortion effects, I filled two rectangles at the far right with a gradient. The **Squeegee** brush from the **F-X** category was used for the top square. **Hurricane**, from the **Distortion** category, and **Shattered** (an F-X variant) were applied to the bottom square.

Brush Tuning

I like using the Piano Keys brush to demonstrate how to change the behavior of a variant using Brush Controls. Open the Brush Creator and choose **Piano Keys** from the **Brush Selector Bar**. With a bright color, make a couple of strokes in the scratch pad area of the Stroke Designer section. Notice the Brush Controls list clearly shows which controls are available for the current variant. All the other controls are grayed out. **General** gives you the most basic info about any variant. As you can see in Figure 7.3, the **Dab Type** for this brush is **Captured**, which means it is an irregular shape or group of pixels, such as a small drawing. The shape in this case is a very thin rectangle. You can get an individual Piano Keys dab on your canvas if you tap your Wacom pen tip on the tablet. The Size control panel also shows the shape of the dab in the Brush Dab Preview window. (If that window shows a circle, tap on it once, and it will show the captured shape.) Figure 7.4 shows the Size control panel and a few single piano keys, along with longer piano passages in the scratch pad.

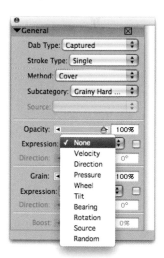

Figure 7.3
Key controls.

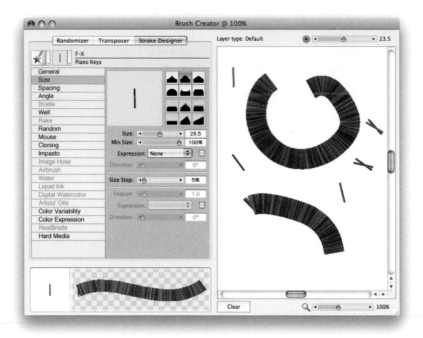

Figure 7.4

Piano keystrokes.

Grab a Dab!

Several other members of the **F-X** category use captured dabs: **Fairy Dust, Fire, Shattered,** and **Squeegee.** Yes, you can make a new and unique brush dab for any variant. Create it, then select it with the **Rectangular Selection** tool. Use the **Capture Dab** command at the top of the popup menu in the **Brush Selector Bar.**

Look at General controls again (refer to Figure 7.3) and notice that **Opacity** is set to 100%, and the **Expression** field shows **None.** This means there can be no variation in opacity within a stroke. Click on the Expression drop-down list to see the choices available for altering opacity. (These are the same choices you get whenever you see the Expression option in any of the Brush Controls sections.) Choose **Pressure,** and make a test stroke. Now your brush can respond to pressure input from your Wacom pen. It's like using the soft pedal on your piano! Figure 7.5 shows strokes with the default settings at the top left and the pressure-responsive strokes on the right.

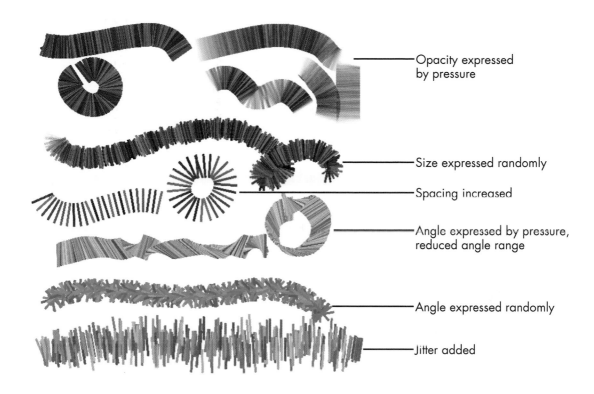

Opacity expressed
by pressure

Size expressed randomly

Spacing increased

Angle expressed by pressure,
reduced angle range

Angle expressed randomly

Jitter added

Figure 7.5
Piano practice.

Piano Keys dabs have no variation in width, and the Size control panel tells you why. The Expression variable to control size is set to None. As if that weren't enough, minimum size is 100%. You can choose to have the width of the stroke vary, but there will be no effect unless you reduce the **Min (minimum) Size** setting. When Min Size is around 40% and Random is chosen for Expression, you get the jagged result in the blue stroke. Let's return to the original settings before we make the next few changes. You don't have to remember what those settings were; just use the **Restore Default Variant** command in the **Brush Selector Bar** pop-up menu.

Let's explore the control panels for **Spacing** and **Angle**, shown in Figure 7.6. Spacing refers to the space between dabs. Raising that value from the default 7% to about 40% gives you the picket fence look shown in purple in Figure 7.5. There are two important things to notice in the **Angle** control panel: the Expression variable is **Direction**, and **Ang(le) Range** is the maximum 360 degrees.

This makes it possible to paint a circle and have all the dabs radiate from the center. What happens if you reduce the **Ang Range** or change the Expression choice to something different? The gold color I used for strokes with **Ang Range** at 180 degrees and **Pressure** used for **Expression** looks a bit like twisted ribbons. The stroke in green is the result of choosing Random for the expression of the full 360 degree angle range.

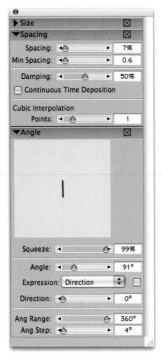

Figure 7.6

Spacing and Angle controls.

Expression: Caffeine

Speaking of random expression, there is a Random section in Brush Controls where you'll find a slider called **Jitter**. The aptly named Nervous Pen has a default Jitter, but you can add Jitter to any brush, as I've done for Piano Keys in blue-green.

Restore the default variant again and open one more control panel, **Color Variability.** The HSV settings show why the color variation in the Piano Keys stroke has darker and lighter shades of very similar colors. Value or Luminosity variation is relatively high at 15%, with Hue variation at only 4% and no Saturation variation at all. Play with those sliders and see what happens.

Spraying Color—or Candy

Look at the Furry Brush strokes in Figure 7.1 again. The General controls for this variant show that the Dab Type is **Line Airbrush.** The stroke does look like a spray of lines, and it behaves like members of the Airbrush category in a couple of ways. The spray is directional, depending on the tilt and bearing of your Wacom pen. Also, the brush keeps spraying even when you're not moving it. That feature is called **Continuous Time Deposition,** and you can see it enabled in the **Spacing** control panel. Can you guess what the HSV Color Variability settings are?

How do you paint with jelly beans, mints, and other tasty treats? The amazing **Image Hose** can spray not only junk food, but tiny images of any kind. The content is determined by your choice in the **Nozzle Selector,** available at the bottom-right corner of the Toolbox. Like all libraries (paper, gradients, patterns, and so on), you can load a different collection and reshuffle the items between libraries with the Mover utility. Now take a look at the variant list for the Image Hose category, shown in Figure 7.7. Here's where you decide whether you want image bits scattered around or marching in a line, and whether to use pressure (P) direction (D), randomness (R), or other variables to control the size or angle of the images.

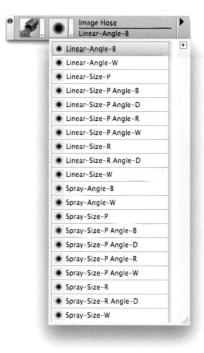

Figure 7.7

You can spray that again.

Load the custom library, **Rhoda Nozzles**, and practice using some of these techniques. My **Image Hose** sampler, shown in Figure 7.8, uses the following nozzles and variants:

- **Seashells:** Spray-Size-P

- **Koi:** Spray-Size-P Angle D

- **Nuts and bolts:** Linear-Size-P Angle-D

- **Candy:** Linear-Size-R

- **Sushi:** Linear-Size-P

Those sushi slices on the left are too close together. How would you increase the spacing to display the center of each piece better? As for the single slice on the far right—that was done by tapping the tablet once, using a variant that did not specify size changes so that any amount of pressure would produce a full-sized sushi.

Is there a practical use for painting with patterns, gradients, and pieces of food? Our next project should help answer that question.

Figure 7.8
Spray that sushi!

Experimental Self-Portrait

Artists have drawn and painted themselves since the invention of the mirror. Even when van Gogh couldn't afford to hire a model, his own face was always handy. Portraits don't necessarily have to be restricted to head and shoulders, and they certainly don't have to be realistic. Begin with a recent photo of yourself, but don't expect it to look much like you at the end. We'll be mixing media with a vengeance, and I'll introduce you to several more of Painter's features and tools.

Be Yourself

I'll be working with the image shown in Figure 7.9, which has a warm *chiaroscuro* look. No, that's not an Italian dessert, but the way Rembrandt created form by having light emerge from shadow. By the time I'm finished, it won't look much like a Rembrandt—more like Picasso on a bad day.

Make a Quick Clone of the photo and open the **Auto-Painting** palette. Turn Smart Stroke Painting off, as shown in Figure 7.10, so you can choose from a wide array of stroke styles.

Figure 7.9
Rembrandt van Rhoda.

Figure 7.10
Get smart.

133

I generally prefer to apply my own brushstrokes one at a time, but I'll make an exception for the Auto-Painting feature. We'll make frequent changes in the stroke style and Cloner variant, starting and stopping every few seconds. Painter's random placement of strokes will add an abstract quality.

Work with tracing paper off so you can see only the splats, scribbles, hatches, and zigzags (yes, that's what they're called) pop onto the canvas. Choose Cloner variants like Graffiti Cloner, Flat Oil Cloner, Fine Gouache Cloner, and Impressionist Cloner. Hit the **Play** button at the bottom of the **Auto-Painting** palette, and watch your painting take shape. Hit **Stop** after a few seconds, and if you don't like the result, use the Undo command. For maximum variety, switch to a different stroke and Cloner variant before you hit Play again. If there are some combinations you like better than others, repeat them. Don't let the process go too far, making sure that quite a bit of white space remains. Figure 7.11 shows an early state, where only my mouth is recognizable amid all the squiggles and dabs. By the time my eye was revealed, as shown in Figure 7.12, I was ready to quit. Save this stage and turn your attention to the original photo again.

Figure 7.11
Too abstract.

Figure 7.12
Close enough.

Borrowing Features

Open the **Image Portfolio**, a library of small images that can be dragged onto your canvas where each will reside on its own layer. Load the custom image library called **FaceParts.por,** shown in Figure 7.13. This is a collection of eyes, noses, and mouths I have scanned from magazines or found on the Internet. Use these or find your own using Google image searches. Better yet, use your own facial features from several other photos (safer than risking rejection from transplanting others' digital body parts).

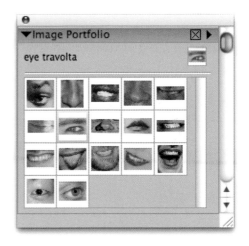

Figure 7.13
Name that nose!

Whose Face Is It Anyway?

If you include bits and pieces of other people's faces in your own creations, be careful. This is not usually a problem unless you want to make a profit from somebody else's image. See the Appendix for a discussion of copyrights and similar matters.

Drag a new mouth, nose, eye, or all three onto your photo. These features will be easy to resize, rotate, or distort with the new **Transform** features in Painter 11. Figure 7.14 shows a nice fresh eye in the process of being manipulated with the tools shown in Figure 7.15. Save this version in RIF format, keeping the new face parts on their own layers.

Figure 7.14
Rhoda gets an eye job.

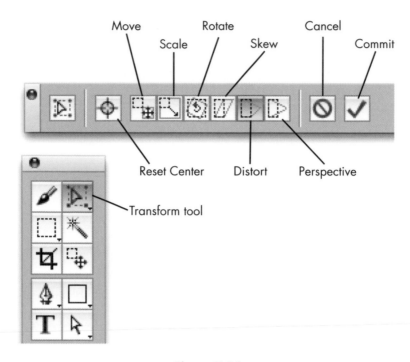

Figure 7.15

Transformation information.

P.S., I Love You

Emulating the "industry standard" (Photoshop) at last, the Transform tool in Painter 11 brings a welcome relief from the clunky Orientation tools of prior versions. Like Photoshop, the Edit menu now offers a Free Transform command for combining all maneuvers.

Layer Masks

Ready to combine both the Auto-Painting and the face transplant? Return to the Auto-Painting image and choose **Select > All and Edit > Copy**. Then **Edit > Paste** it onto the layered image, and drag the new layer under the face parts. Try various composite methods. I chose the **Screen** composite method for a pleasing blend that wasn't too dark. Figure 7.16 shows this version.

Figure 7.16
Facial reconstruction.

Suppose you want to have more control over how to combine layers. You can actually paint out parts of a layer nondestructively (you can change your mind at any time) using a layer mask. I created a layer mask for the Auto-Painting by clicking on the icon shown in Figure 7.17.

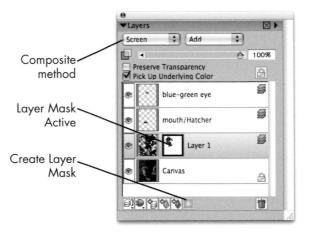

Figure 7.17
Faux erasing.

Use black to paint on the parts you want to be invisible. If you change your mind later, bring back the "erased" pixels by painting with white on the layer mask. I wanted to reveal some of the elements on the canvas layer in a scribbled style, so I used rough strokes with a Pencil variant. The detail in Figure 7.18 shows that the nose, right eye, and cap are more visible. Refer to Figure 7.17 again and notice the layer mask area shows where those black strokes were made.

Figure 7.18
Scribble on the mask.

Another Black Mark for You

If you're trying to paint invisibility into the layer but you get black strokes on the image, it's because you're painting on the image, not on the mask. Click on the icon you want in the Layers palette. A heavy black border shows which one is active.

Over the Top

I haven't forgotten to bring in some of the special brushes we examined at the beginning of the chapter. Make a new layer and, if necessary, drag it to the top of the stack. Turn off the visibility of other layers so you can see the canvas clearly while you paint. Use either a Grad Pen or the Pattern Pen Masked to draw a simple outline of your face on the new layer. I used the Pattern Pen Masked with **Silver Tubing** for the drawing shown in Figure 7.19. To blend it with the other layers, I switched to the **Hard Light** method and "erased" some parts using a new layer mask.

Figure 7.19
Pattern Pen outline.

Make another layer for working with the Image Hose. I sprayed **Gardenias** from the default library on one side of the face and **Nuts 'n' Bolts** from the **Rhoda Nozzles** collection on the other side, suggesting a feminine/masculine contrast. This time Luminosity was the composite method that seemed to work best. I went back to painting black on the Auto-Painting layer mask to bring in more of the canvas layer on the dark side of the face, this time using the **Variable Splatter** Airbrush. Figure 7.20 shows this stage. It's nearly done, but first I'll have to teach you a very sweet technique.

Figure 7.20
Something's missing.

Painting with Chocolate

Welcome to yet another unique set of special effects, the **Dynamic** plug-ins. They reside at the bottom of the Layers palette and have an electric plug icon. Choose **Liquid Metal** from the popup list, with a glance at some of the other choices for future reference. You may recall our brief visit to Bevel World in Lesson 6.

Figure 7.21 shows the **Liquid Metal** dialog box (which must remain open while you are creating Liquid Metal effects) and the new layer (Liquid Metal Floater 1) made automatically to accommodate those strokes. Practice making some strokes with the brush icon selected, and switch to the circle icon to make metallic droplets. Notice the tendency for droplets to attract each other and run together! The Undo command won't work here, so if you want to remove a stroke or a droplet, use the arrow icon to select it and then press the **Delete/Backspace** key. Strokes are actually made up of a sequence of droplets. You can see them individually by enabling **Display Handles** in the Liquid Metal dialog. Even after you click OK, a plug-in layer remains dynamic—that is, you can access the original controls by simply double-clicking the item in the Layers palette. You can choose **Convert to Default Layer** from the Layers palette popup menu if you need to apply other brushes and effects. Figure 7.22 shows some test strokes and droplets.

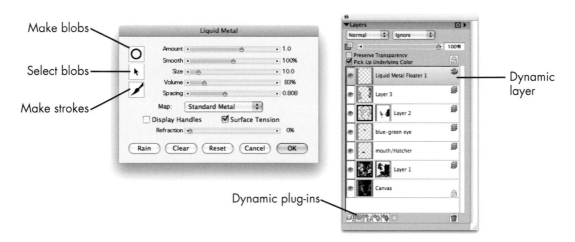

Figure 7.21
Dynamic duo.

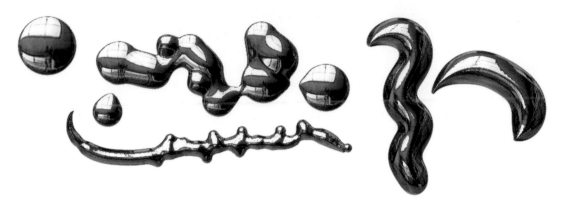

Figure 7.22
Droplets and strokes.

Liquid Metal, along with several other Dynamic plug-ins, was introduced in Painter 5, and it is still amazing! With a little tweaking of
the controls and preparing alternate source images for the reflection
map, you can emulate a variety of liquids, including melted chocolate!

Consider the Sauce

Notice that Clone Source is available as an alternative to the default
Standard Metal in the Map list. Recall that you can specify any
open image as a Clone Source using the File menu. In order to
have a Clone Source that will imitate chocolate, I created an image
called **Chocolate_source.jpg**, shown in Figure 7.23, along with the
Gradient settings I used. This image is available in the Lesson 7

folder on the CD, but it's easy to
make from scratch. Choose a dark
chocolate for your primary color
and a milk chocolate for the secondary color. Make a new canvas
500 pixels square and fill it with
the two-point gradient using the
Spiral style and one of the double
configurations at the bottom of the
Gradients palette. Click inside your
canvas with the Paint Bucket. For
smoothing the spiral edges, use
Effects > Focus > Soften.

Figure 7.23
Brown on brown.

Choose your chocolate gradient image from the **File > Clone Source** list. Make a new blank canvas for practice and launch the **Liquid Metal** palette. Choose **Clone Source** from the **Map** drop-down list and paint with any combination of strokes and droplets. Switch back to Standard Metal to compare the effects. My effort is shown in Figure 7.24. Click OK when you're finished. Return to your self-portrait project and create a Liquid Metal layer or two. You can double-click a Dynamic layer at any time to make changes in the strokes, blobs, or map.

Figure 7.24
How bittersweet it is!

fear of Commitment?

When you apply any effect to a plug-in layer, or when you attempt to paint on it with a brush variant, you'll have to commit it to a standard layer. If you commit, the electric plug icon for the layer is replaced by the default layer icon, and you can no longer make dynamic changes.

Icing on the Cake

With a couple of Liquid Metal strokes for eyeglasses, and several Liquid Chocolate strokes on another layer for hair (separate layers are needed if you want to use different image maps), changes can be viewed in Figure 7.25. Yes, it is a bit overwrought, but I can always simplify by minimizing some elements or even eliminating them altogether. The most successful version was probably way back in Figure 7.12, but that would make for a very short chapter, and you would have missed out on all kinds of fun. The process of comparing alternative versions with different layers turned off, switched to another composite method, Opacity setting, or dragged to another position in the stack can give you hours of pleasure—or confusion.

Figure 7.25
Quit when you're a head!

What's Next?

After feasting on this smorgasbord, you may be overstuffed and need some time to digest everything. Maybe even take a nap! Many of these special brushes are pretty spicy and might not be to your taste. Or you may find that some of the features are best used as a seasoning or a garnish, just a sprinkle to add zest to the dish. I could probably push this food metaphor for a few more courses, but I'll just suggest a little chilled sorbet to cleanse your. . . palette!

There are still some amazing areas of Painter we haven't explored, and that journey isn't over yet. But for the next lesson, we'll get back to basics again—the basics of drawing and painting.

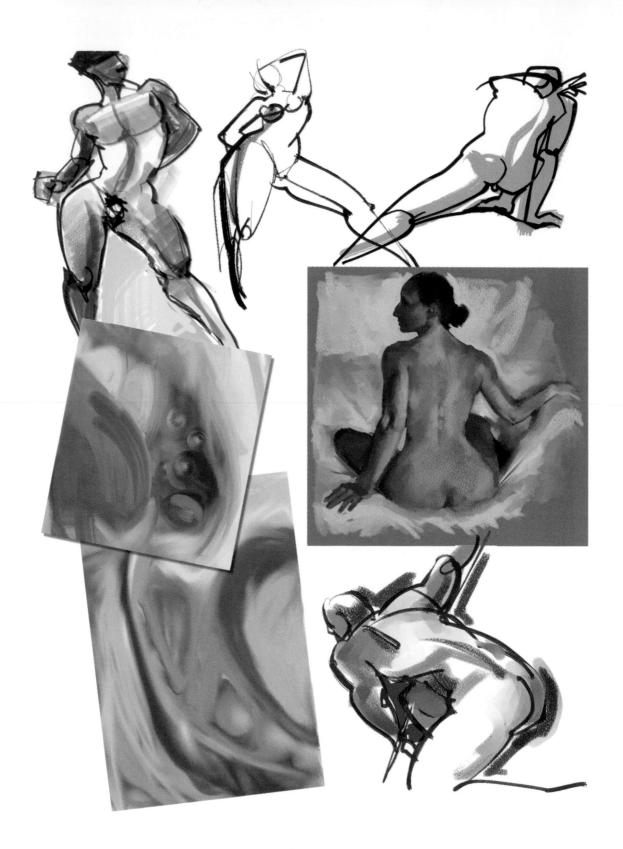

8 fine Art Challenges

Whether in action or repose, clothed or nude, classically rendered or abstract, drawings and paintings of the human body are the most popular subject matter for students as well as accomplished masters. The challenge in figure drawing is making your work look like the subject. The challenge in abstract art is making your work not look like the subject or (depending on your definition of abstract) not even having a subject. You'll have the opportunity to do both in this set of lessons.

Figure Drawing

In a typical figure drawing class or workshop, an undraped model poses for increasing lengths of time, beginning with very short "gesture" poses lasting only a minute or two. Short poses are very energetic and exciting to capture quickly with a few strokes. For many years, I worked with charcoal or oil pastels on big (18x24-inch) sheets of paper. Nowadays, I'm usually the only one showing up with a laptop and Wacom tablet. My hands stay clean, and I don't have to worry about where to store all those drawings.

Find someone willing to pose for you, not necessarily naked. Or take your laptop and tablet to a figure drawing workshop. As a last resort, use photos from the **People > Figure Study** folder on the CD.

Quick Study

Figure 8.1 shows two digital gesture sketches I did in about four minutes each. They are samples from a recent figure drawing workshop where I gave some of Painter 11's **Real** variants a test drive. There are more examples from this session (and others) on the CD that accompanies this book.

Figure 8.1
Four-minute poses.

I'm rapidly becoming addicted to the **Real Soft Pastel** and **Real 6B Soft Pencil**. They are just two of the awesome variants that allow you to draw wide shading strokes by holding your Wacom pen at an extreme angle, as shown in Figure 8.2. The top row of strokes in Figure 8.3 were made with the Real 6B Soft Pencil. Next are strokes using the Real Soft Pastel. Marks at the bottom are from the **Sharp Marker**, which is only sharp when you hold it upright.

Figure 8.2

Extreme drawing hand.

Figure 8.3

Getting real.

Naked Truth

Being forced to work this quickly encourages you to focus on the essence of the pose, skipping details. Just as important, this kind of practice helps you plunge into the process and ignore any self-doubt about your skill. After all, gesture drawings aren't meant to look good, and even if your effort sucks, there's another fresh opportunity to be successful every couple of minutes! "Process, not product" is the mantra you need to repeat to yourself if you are judging your work negatively or you feel "stuck."

There are some exercises you can do to loosen up and other methods to develop accuracy. Let's combine a couple of them. A classic technique for practicing eye-hand coordination is *blind contour* drawing. The idea is to keep your pen or drawing tool on the paper or tablet and, *without looking at your work* (that's the blind part), slowly and deliberately make an outline of the subject. Whether it's a vase or a nude model, the process is the same, and improvement *will happen* if you practice.

I'll put a spin on blind contour drawing and recommend *blind gesture* drawing. Do *not* be slow and deliberate, and do *not* attempt to follow the outer edge of the subject. So, all we're keeping is the "blind" part. Figure 8.4 shows a few blind gestures made very quickly (green shading and pink background added later). After doing several of these, you'll be amazed at what you can accomplish with your eyes open!

Figure 8.4
Flying blind.

Do you have some favorite brush variants you tend to rely on over and over? I suggest you try a few brushes that are less familiar. Avoid the special effects brushes for now, and stick with natural media categories. A category I generally ignore, partly because I don't know how to pronounce it, is **Sumi-e.** These brushes imitate the effect of Chinese bamboo brushes. Figure 8.5 shows some test strokes with a few Sumi-e variants.

A Method to My Madness

The Sumi-e category includes a **Dry Ink** variant, which differs from the one in the **Calligraphy** group: The method is **Buildup** rather than **Cover.** Test what happens when you change between those two methods in the General control panel of the Brush Controls in the Brush Creator.

Figure 8.5
Bamboo brushes.

Here's a checklist to help you prepare for a digital figure drawing session so you can work efficiently with minimal distractions:

- Use the **Brush Tracker** in Painter **Preferences** to reset pressure sensitivity to your touch.

- Make a custom palette with the variants and textures you want to use. One of my figure drawing brush palettes, shown in Figure 8.6, is available in the Pals & Libs folder on the CD.

- Create at least one template canvas with the size and color background you want, with a layer in **Gel** or Multiply mode to keep color separate from your line work.

- If you're working from photos, open at least 10 of them at once so you don't lose your concentration when doing fast gesture warm-ups.

- Use the **Iterative Save** function so you don't have to create new names for successive drawings.

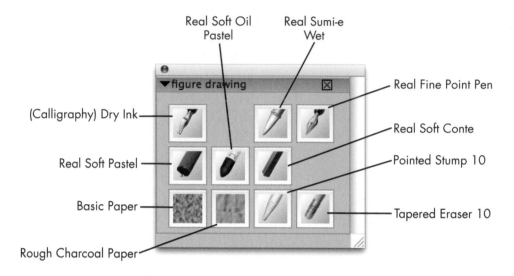

Figure 8.6
Some suggestions.

Work for 20 minutes at a stretch, first with a series of 10 two-minute warm-ups, followed by four five-minute sketches, then two ten-minute drawings. Use any style(s) and brushes you like—just don't trace!

Long Pose

We'll use **seated_nude.jpg,** shown in Figure 8.7, to develop a chalk/pastel drawing of Rasa through several stages.

Figure 8.7
Classic pose.

Enhance the photo by using my settings in the **Underpainting** palette, as shown in Figure 8.8. I started with the **Classical Color Scheme**, which made the image much too dark, so I brightened it and reduced the color saturation. A **Smart Blur** provided just the right softness. I saved this version and later decided the contrast was a bit too harsh, so I pasted it onto the original as a new layer and turned the opacity down to 60%. This **seated_nude_classic.jpg**, shown in Figure 8.9, is what we'll use for our model.

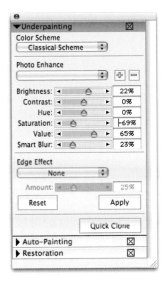

Figure 8.8
Show us your underpaints.

Figure 8.9
Classic colors.

What's My Gamut?

The subtle shadows on the nude at this stage look much better on screen than on the printed page. Bright colors can also be a challenge to reproduce in a book. For an insight as to why that happens, see the "Show Us Your Gamuts" section in the Appendix.

Getting Organized

Make a new canvas the same size as the prepared photo (875x864 pixels) and choose a warm medium gray for the paper color. To match my color exactly, switch to the RGB Sliders setting in the Paper Color Picker, shown in Figure 8.10, and enter Red 132, Green 117, and Blue 117. This color is just a bit redder than a neutral gray, which would have equal amounts of Red, Green, and Blue components.

Work with the prepared photo and your toned canvas side by side, at the same magnification. Make a new Color Set from the photo. To maximize screen space, close all palettes except your custom brush palette and the Color Set, and place these two items in the positions you like. Save this layout in the Arrange Palettes menu.

Figure 8.10
RGB settings.

Proportional Response

To imitate a traditional figure drawing environment, we won't use layers, and tracing is absolutely forbidden! You can use a grid to check accuracy once or twice, but the whole idea is to improve your skill at observation and self-correction. Working from general to specific, you'll erase or smear out lines you don't need as you gradually improve and refine the drawing. That's the basic plan. Let's see how it goes.

Start with a quick gesture, as shown in Figure 8.11. Use a large chalk or pastel, such as **Square Hard Pastel 40**, for blocking in the most basic elements of the pose in a few strokes. We could use this as the first stage of our long drawing, but I'll just consider it a preliminary warm-up.

Figure 8.12 shows another way to begin (rough patches of color made with a large pastel), with special attention to indicating the lightest and darkest areas of the composition.

Figure 8.11
Blocky gesture.

I was serious when I told you not to trace for this project, but don't worry—there are things Painter can do to help with your observations. **Grids** and **Guides**, found in the **Canvas** menu, are useful for lining up parts of the figure and judging angles. Set up the **Grid Options** so the lines are 150 pixels apart. The photo in Figure 8.13 is faded so you can clearly see the lines that indicate relative sizes and positions of key points on the pose. In this pose, Rasa is four heads high, measuring to the tips of her fingers. The vertical line shows how various body points line up, and the angled lines give additional guides for checking accuracy. Notice that the top of her head lines up with her elbow and the tip of her collar bone. The upper edge of her right hand is on the same horizontal line as the point where her arm meets her torso. Another horizontal lineup is her left elbow and right knee. You will use these kinds of comparisons often as you work.

Figure 8.12
Some rough patches.

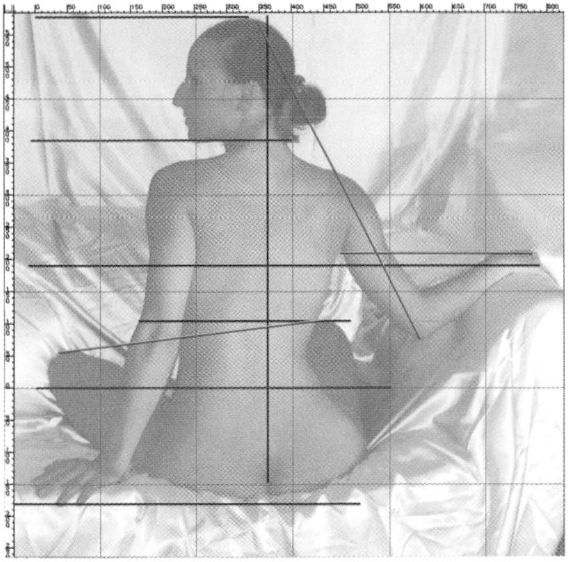

Figure 8.13
Girl grid.

Rule of Thumb

In a traditional setting, the artist makes comparative measurements by sighting along his or her outstretched hand, using a pencil or (as in a cartoon parody) the thumb. Let's say the model's head is one thumb length. How many thumb lengths is it to her elbow or knee?

With the grid turned on, I can see where my drawing needs correction, and I've made some with the dark contour lines shown in Figure 8.14. We are on a journey of discovery to find the lines, tones, and colors that will describe the form.

Figure 8.14
Finding contours.

Continue to observe and correct the contour. The proportions must be right before you begin to work on details. Bring the entire image along at about the same pace, not just one area at a time. Draw the negative shapes around Rasa's face and between her torso and limbs with light colors. Figure 8.15 shows the right arm working much better, and tonal modeling has begun to suggest the solidity and weight of the figure.

Figure 8.15
Develop slowly.

Lighter flesh tones have been added to the drawing in Figure 8.16. Become aware of color temperature—warm reds and yellows of the skin in contrast to the cool grays and greens of the satin sheets.

Build up thin layers of pigment gradually, and use a **Smudge** tool, such as the **Pointed Stump**, to gently blend skin tones, but don't smooth things out too much.

Anatomically Correct

An understanding of how bones and muscles fit together will certainly give you a leg up in drawing the figure convincingly. But even if you don't know a *latissimus dorsi* from your *gluteus maximus*, careful observation will take you pretty far.

Figure 8.16
Flesh it out.

Figure 8.17
Firm it up.

Can you see which parts of the drawing in Figure 8.17 are working better than other areas? That's a question to ask yourself frequently as you work. It might help to squint your eyes so you reduce detail and just check on the values. Even better, get up out of your chair and go to the other side of the room to evaluate your image.

In Figure 8.18, the planes of the face and muscles of the back are more developed, and the left arm is possibly overdeveloped. How would you trim down that heavy forearm? (Hint: Notice the distance of the arm from the hip.)

When you have enough colors in the image, use the **Dropper** tool to sample a color you want to use again. It's also efficient to have your Color Set swatches use LHS sort order, so the colors are organized first by lightness, as in Figure 8.19. It's easy to find a lighter color just by choosing a swatch lower in the set.

Figure 8.18
Muscles and planes.

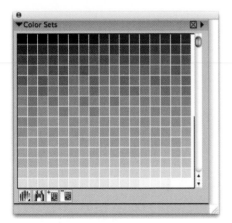

Figure 8.19
Lighter is lower.

There is just enough of the satin drapery in Figure 8.20 to provide information about the sofa Rasa is sitting on. The important elements of the satin, in my opinion, are the reflection of flesh tones from her arm and the tension lines from her hip to the arm of the sofa. We also have described the left hand reasonably well. A few strokes with the **Blender Stump** remove the dark lines under her buttocks to make it appear that she is sitting on a soft surface. A small **Pastel** variant, like the 3-pixel **Pastel Pencil,** is ideal for details at this point.

Figure 8.20
Satin finish.

Figure 8.21 shows a close-up of the upper half of my drawing along with the photo for comparison. I set the grid lines to 100 pixels apart. Although the left elbow and right knee are pretty good in relation to each other, they are both too high. Minor errors in the proportions of the face are more important, so I'll fix those.

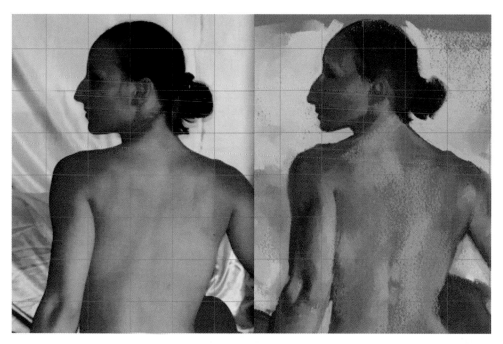

Figure 8.21
Double checking.

In real life, I'd have to erase or wipe out the areas needing correction and then paint them all over again. But I'm in a hurry to get to the next lesson, so I'll "cheat" just a little. I used the Lasso tool to select Rasa's facial features, as shown in Figure 8.22.

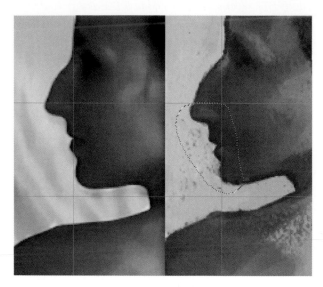

Figure 8.22
Face time.

I moved the selection a few pixels up and to the right, using the keyboard arrows to "nudge" the selection one pixel at a time. Figure 8.23 shows the results. That curved gray shape is the paper color, of course. I can sample the creamy green and light gray colors around it with the Dropper tool and paint it out. Those colors can also be used with the Pastel Pencil to reshape Rasa's nose and smooth her jaw line. Refer to the illustration at the beginning of this chapter for the final version.

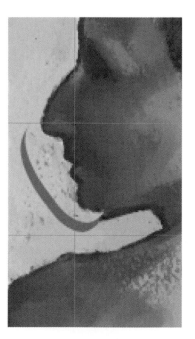

Figure 8.23
Nudge the nose.

Abstract Painting

And now for something completely different. No careful measuring required, and no way to tell when you're done or even how well you're doing. I'll leave you to explore the history of abstract art movements on your own—Wikipedia would be a good start. You won't need to know anything about specific artists or styles in this section, but it will be helpful to keep a few basic concepts in mind. The essential elements for creating art of any kind are as follows:

- **Line**: So many possibilities—straight or curved, smooth or jagged, bold or nervous (I could go on)...

- **Shape**: Large or small, geometric or organic, simple or complex...

- **Tone (color)**: Dark or light, saturated or dull, warm or cool...

- **Texture**: Rough or smooth, subtle or strong, natural or synthetic...

So there are a lot of choices you can make for each of those four "simple" elements. And the categories can overlap: a line that curves back on itself or is really fat becomes a shape, lots of lines close together make a texture, and so on. Then you need to work out how to organize them on your canvas. A few principles, in no particular order, will help with that:

- **Contrast**: Not just tonal differences, but contrast in size or texture or complexity of elements creates visual interest.

- **Repetition**: Create unity by repeating some of the elements, with variation in size, color, or angle.

- **Balance**: Composition, or the placement of elements so that they work well within the picture plane.

- **Focal Point**: Create at least one center of interest so it's not just wallpaper.

Variations on a Theme

Begin with an existing image or a set of related images—just about any subject will do. There are several photos in the Things folder on the CD that are nearly abstract already, so it will be like "painting fish in a barrel," if you get my drift. I put about a dozen of them into a folder called Abstract This!

The goal is to create a painting that refers to the subject of the photo and borrows freely from its visual elements, but then goes off in its own direction. I'll work with the series of photos in the Dental Work folder, one of which is shown in Figure 8.24. The photographer is Dr. Leo Arellano, DDS, and he was wearing rubber gloves and a mask at the time these shots were taken. I made a quick trip-tych, shown in Figure 8.25, combining three pairs of the photos using the colorful and dramatic **Difference** composite method. It might not be art, but at least I get to deduct my dental work as a business expense.

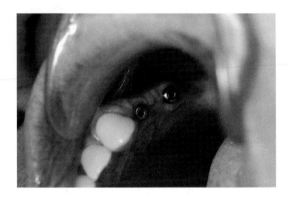

Figure 8.24
Don't forget to floss.

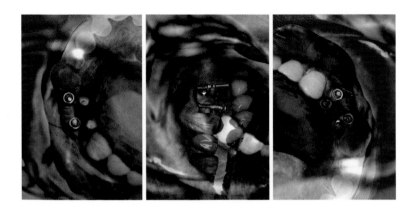

Figure 8.25
Triptych to the dentist!

To keep the enormous number of choices under control, let's work with the left panel of the triptych. I'll use the naming system I started years ago when Dr. Arellano was constructing my bridgework. Open the layered **mouthscape2009.rif**. The individual photos are shown side by side in Figure 8.26. There is a good range of value here, and some contrast in texture as well as in the amount of detail. The repetition of similar shapes and curves makes the two images compatible.

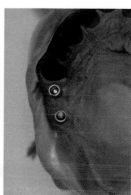

Figure 8.26
Elemental dental.

The colors resulting from the Difference composite method in the triptych are a little garish, so let's try some other techniques. Clone mouthscape2009.rif, which automatically drops the layer into the canvas. Make a duplicate of the composite image on its own layer—copy and paste will do the trick. Apply **Effects > Surface Control > Quick Warp** to the layer copy, using the settings shown in Figure 8.27.

Apply a **Sketchbook Color Scheme** from the **Underpainting** palette to the canvas. Use the **Screen** composite method for the layer. The result should look like Figure 8.28, with soft pastel shades and a bit more complexity and depth from the warped layer.

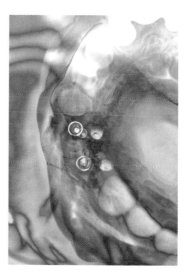

Figure 8.28
Now spit.

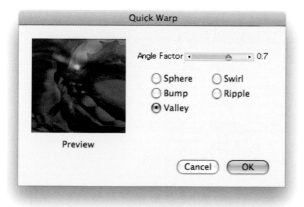

Figure 8.27
Warp factor 7.

Now for some creative smearing. Save this version and clone it so you can enjoy the "smear without fear" experience. The **Water Rake Blender** might be a good choice here. I also recommend **Grainy Mover 40** from the **Distortion** group. Smooth out some areas, but leave other parts with texture details, especially near the focal point of the metal implants. The version in Figure 8.29 already looks like a painting, not just a photo composite.

Did you notice that the focal point is exactly in the center of the image? Not as interesting as putting it elsewhere, based on the Divine Proportion theory (see Lesson 4 for Divine Proportion basics). If we choose the upper-left portrait orientation in the Divine Proportion palette, we can clone the metal bits into the desired spot. In the service of repetition, we'll leave them in the original position as well.

We'll use point-to-point cloning. Choose the **Rubber Stamp** tool and **Option/Alt+click** in the center of the metal implants on the clone source (the previous version of the artwork). Now release the modifier key and begin painting on the position you determined with the Divine Proportion tool. The results are shown in Figure 8.30.

For the finishing touches, let's paint some strokes with **RealBristle Brushes** or **Artists' Oils,** which are capable of painting with more than one color at a time. Recall using the Color Mixer to load these brushes with multiple colors. (Review Lesson 5 for Mixer palette basics.) Create a **Mixer** pad with the major colors from the image blending roughly into each other so you can sample them with the multi-color dropper. I painted some curves and arcs with **Real Oils Short** and decided I was done when I got to the version in Figure 8.31. The lower-left section of the illustration opening this chapter has other paintings from my mouthscape2009 series.

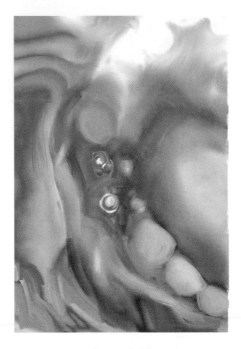

Figure 8.29
No visible gum line.

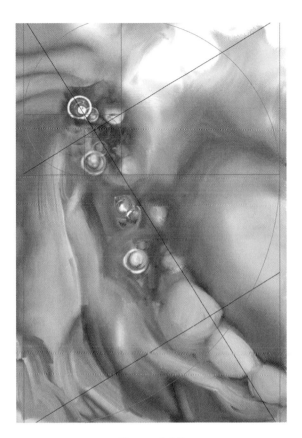

Figure 8.30
Your mouth is divine!

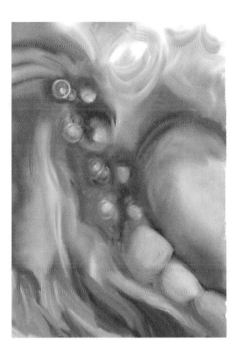

Figure 8.31
Come back in six months.

What's Next?

Congratulations on making it through an intense lesson requiring you to stretch your skills and imagination. I invite you to come back and repeat some of these projects again with different source images. Take your best paintings from this session and print them on canvas or watercolor paper specially made for desktop inkjet printers. If you want to produce large output, see the "Resource" section in the Appendix.

In the next lesson, you'll become an animator.

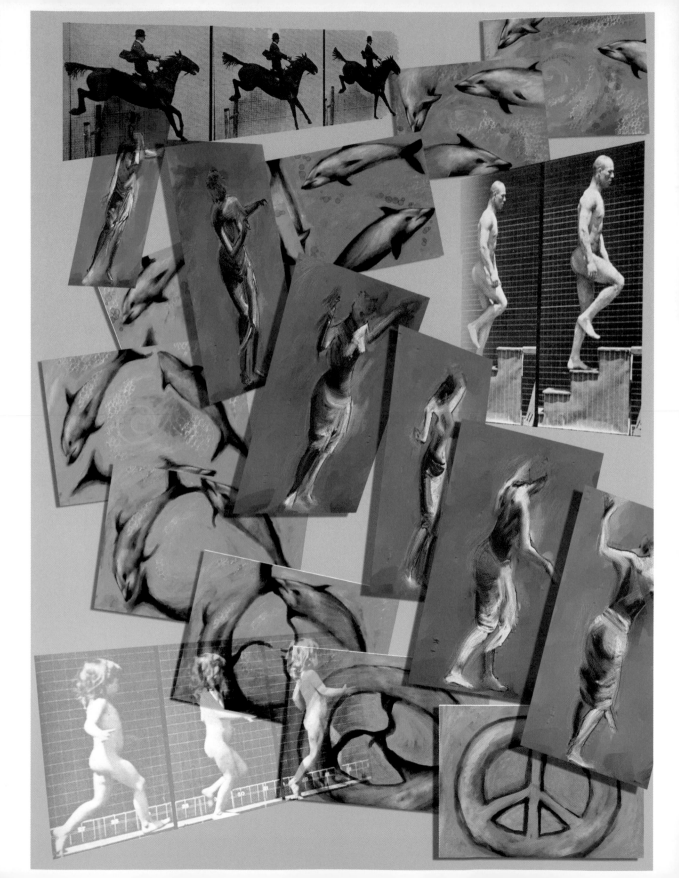

9 Pixel-Based Animation

You've seen the incredible power that Corel Painter has for imitating traditional drawing and painting media. It shouldn't astonish you that Painter can also imitate traditional animation. I'm referring to the time-honored techniques that required drawing and painting by hand on transparent sheets of acetate, or *cels*, which were then photographed by a special camera. Even a short cartoon created in this way can involve teams of specialists for preliminary storyboarding, character design, pencil testing, "tweening" (the job of "inbetweener" involves creating all the frames needed between key frames), inking and painting—well, you get the idea.

On a much smaller scale, you can do all of that using Painter's frame stacks. The Onion Skin feature serves the function of cels, allowing you to see two or more frames at a time so you can manage the necessary amount of change between frames. That's the essence of animation—creating a series of images with slight changes between them so that a rapid viewing of the sequence fools the eye into seeing movement.

You'll be happy to know there are shortcuts and ways to automate some of the work to take a lot of tedious repetition off your hands. Also, there are many styles of experimental animation (without cartoon characters!) that can be created quickly. When you're done, you can save your frame stack in a variety of video or movie formats, including GIF animations for the web.

Digital Cel Basics

Let's set up a blank frame stack and make a quick animation of a worm crossing from one edge of the frame to the other. (The process will be quick, but the worm can travel at various speeds.) Choose **File > New** and enter a convenient size, say 7 inches wide by 5 inches high (or whatever it is in the metric system for the rest of the civilized world), at screen resolution, and choose a paper color other than white—but don't click OK yet. Notice the option at the bottom of the dialog box for a Movie instead of an Image. Click on the **Movie** button and enter 10 in the **Frames** field for a very short movie. With a light blue paper color selected, these settings are shown in Figure 9.1.

When you click OK, you'll be prompted to name your movie and decide where to put it. With that handled, one more decision is presented: How many layers of Onion Skin do you want? Accept the default minimum of 2 and the default storage type.

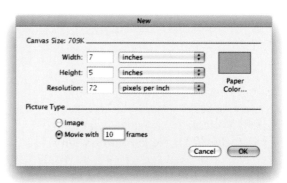

Figure 9.1

New movie.

Painter will create the 10-frame stack to your specifications, and the **Frame Stacks** palette will appear. You'll use this to navigate between frames and (with the **Playback** slider) determine the speed of the animation in frames per second (fps). Figure 9.2 displays the Frame Stacks palette with two frames visible at once, because we chose two layers of Onion Skin. All frames have the blue paper color I chose. Frame 1 is ready for you to work on, as indicated by the red triangle above it.

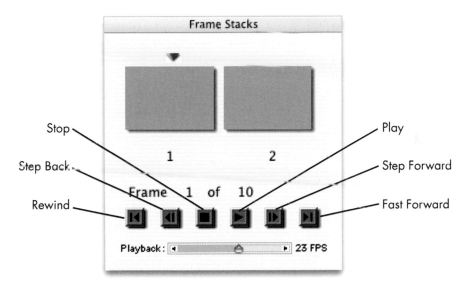

Figure 9.2
Short stack.

Start with a Worm

What brush variants are good for drawing a worm? How about the **Gradient Repeat Pen**? The **Furry Brush** from the **F-X** category (maybe with a size reduction)? I'll use the **Barbed Wire Pen**. Make some practice strokes on frame 1, and customize your brush as desired. Then delete or undo your test strokes in the usual way, or use the **Erase Frame** command in the **Movie** menu.

You Have Been Erased!

The **Erase Frame** command removes all marks and restores a fresh background (paper color) to the frame, but **Delete Frame** removes the frame from the stack altogether, reducing the total number of frames.

Let's plunge right in without any planning—my favorite approach to most projects. Well, maybe we should have a very simple plan: Make the worm enter on the left and exit at the right. So the first stroke on frame 1 is just a little bit of the worm's "head" poking out from the edge of the frame. Step forward to frame 2 and turn on tracing paper, either by clicking its icon at the upper-right edge of your image window or by using **Cmd/Ctrl+T**. Now you can see the slightly less opaque Onion Skin image from frame 1 to use as a reference for the next brush stroke. Make that second stroke overlapping the first one but coming out into the frame a bit more. You'll be estimating how much overlap there should be between strokes in order to come out at the right edge in frame 10. If your worm gets to the right edge before the end of the movie, you can eliminate the empty frames with the **Delete Frames** command in the **Movie** menu. If your worm can't make it to the finish line in 10 frames, make additional blank frames by simply clicking the **Step Forward** button on the **Frame Stacks** palette.

Make the worm wiggle across the frame by giving each brush stroke a slight curve, and alternate the direction of the curves from one frame to the next. Figure 9.3 shows my frame stack with frame 8 active and tracing paper on, so both frame 8 and the previous frame are visible. Play the movie at any point while you're working so you can check for any problems (like an early bird waiting to swoop down for a fuzzy snack). Notice that the movie automatically loops over and over, so the worm will keep reappearing at the left edge and tirelessly make his way offstage again and again. My wiggly worm is available for you to examine or edit in the Lesson 9 folder on the CD. There are several other Painter movies there to demonstrate other projects in this lesson, or just for fun.

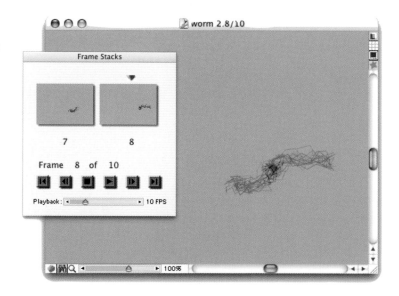

Figure 9.3
Maybe it's a caterpillar.

You Can Play That Again!

Painter movies are automatically saved as frame stacks, uncompressed files that can get huge in a hurry. Our one-second worm is a 7MB file, so a one-minute movie with the same frame dimensions would be (let's see now) 420MB! You'll want to use the **Save As** options: **QuickTime** (on the Mac platform) and **AVI** (for the PC) are formats that enable viewing your movies with your favorite player utility. The files can be compressed enough to share with friends via email attachments. With the compression settings I chose, that 7MB worm got trimmed down to a petite 32KB.

After this quick-n-dirty trial run, you can imagine the potential for creating longer frame stacks with more complex drawings and multiple layers of Onion Skin for better control over your animated elements. Hang onto that worm movie in case you want to enhance it later: add a sunrise, a scrolling background, or another critter.

Automating Animating

If that exercise wasn't quick and easy enough for you, here's a labor-saving technique that will allow you to sit back and let Painter divide a brush stroke into the number of frames you want. Just two commands are needed: **Record Stroke** in the Brush Selector Bar popup menu and **Apply Brush Stroke to Movie** in the Movie menu.

Let's add this effect to our worm movie. See, I knew it would come in handy again. Be sure to invoke the Record Stroke command before you make the stroke. I switched to blue for my new worm, and Figure 9.4 shows the brush stroke that's about to be animated. I painted it from right to left, so it will cross the frame going in the opposite direction of our original worm. Yes, the stroke was made on one of the frames of my movie, for convenience, but the Undo command got rid of it. This had no effect on the recording function.

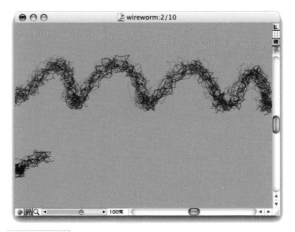

Figure 9.4
The worm turns.

No Turning Back

Changes to a movie can't be undone. Before adding another element to your movie, save it in QuickTime or AVI format, then reopen it and give it a different name. It will expand to a frame stack again, and the original version will be protected. Also, be advised that while you work on a movie, there's no undo available for a frame after you've advanced to another frame.

When the Apply Brush Stroke to Movie command is chosen, my fancy barbed wire stroke becomes a madly bouncing worm rushing past the little red wriggler. Check it out by playing the 2wireworms frame stack.

There's another way to animate a brush stroke that gives you much more control. Right under the Record Stroke command is **Playback Stroke**. This feature lets you repeat a recorded stroke with a single tap of your Wacom pen (or click of your mouse). Playback can save time spent redoing the same stroke frame after frame if the only thing that needs changing is its position. There are some other clever ways to use this feature, such as changing colors and even switching to a different brush variant between taps. To see various ways a single oval stroke can be played back, Figure 9.5 is provided. Can you recognize all the variants used? That smeary effect on the right comes from **Coarse Distorto** in the **Distortion** category, and the distressed area in the center is the work of **Impasto > Acid Etch**. Image Hose sprayed the gardenias in the lower left corner, and Pattern Pen Masked was used with both Double Helix and Silver Tubing. Not a bad way to create an abstract painting, actually.

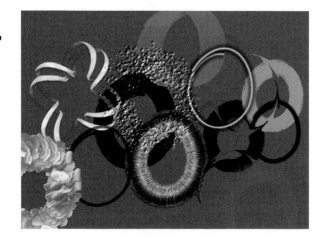

Figure 9.5
Please repeat that.

Working with Layers

If you want to animate an image element that's more complex than a single stroke, create it first or select it from a source image and drag it onto your first movie frame. It will become a layer and can be manipulated like any other layer. Scale it, rotate it, distort it, adjust the colors, or apply any effects you like. When you step forward to the next frame, the layer is merged into the canvas in the previous frame but available for any adjustments in the current frame. Continue from one frame to the next. Be sure to deselect the layer in the final frame.

I grabbed a tomato slice from the **Image Portfolio** and made it fly off into space by using the **Effects / Scale** command and typing in the percentage of size reduction for each position change. (Need a reminder about the Image Portfolio? Look at Lesson 7 again.) My stack of tomato slices can be viewed and edited, or tossed with a nice vinaigrette. The eight frames were saved as numbered files in a folder named **Flying Tomato Files.**

I saved the tomato movie before adding a background. I chose the aptly named **Red Streak** gradient for a background fill. I made the background animate by changing its angle in the Gradients palette with each frame, moving the red button on the **Angle Ring** clockwise. Figure 9.6 shows the Gradients palette, and Figure 9.7 has a frame with Onion Skin turned on, so you can see the previous frame also. The result was a tomato slice flying through a turning spiral. Play the **Tomato Escapes** frame stack. It's not bad, considering the few frames involved and my casual attitude about accurate placement.

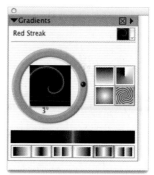

Figure 9.6
Angle.

Stack 'Em Up

Here's how to open a series of images as a frame stack. All images must be the same size and numbered sequentially from 01 or 001 (to accommodate the total number of frames) at the beginning or the end of the file name. Choose **File > Open** and check the **Open Numbered Files** box near the bottom of the dialog box. You'll be prompted to choose the first file in a sequence, then the last file. You'll have to give the frame stack a name. Be sure the file name is unique to protect other movies you may be working on.

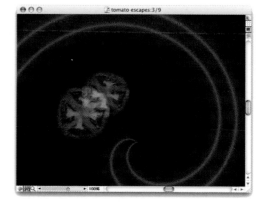

Figure 9.7
Flying tomato.

Dolphins for Peace

Introducing our guest animator, Barbara Pollak. Some frames from her dolphin sequence appear at the beginning of this chapter. The CD that accompanies this book includes a GIF version of her swimming dolphins animation. She'll show you how to create it from scratch without getting seasick. Okay, Barbara, you have the floor.

Thanks, Rhoda. This was a short animation clip I created for a live action movie called *The Source* about women who surf. In this segment, the dolphins swim around and around until they meet and merge to become a peace symbol—very California. Painter was perfect for this project because it allowed me to use brushes and paper textures to create water effects.

My dolphin painting is shown in Figure 9.8, and it's yours to borrow. If you have your own illustration or photo of a fish that is easy to cut out, you are free to use that instead.

Figure 9.8
Flipper.

Fish Story

(Yes, I know they are mammals, but Rhoda wanted a funny heading.) Create a new frame stack by choosing **File > New** and clicking the **Movie** button. Enter **1** in the **Frames** field. This will make sense later. Set the width to 649 pixels, the height to 547 pixels, and choose an ocean blue color: R88, G165, B252. Click OK, name your stack, and decide where to put it. The stack refers to the "raw" file. When it comes time to play back the animation (as part of a web site, for example), you will save the animation in another format, such as GIF.

Open the **dolphin.tiff** image. Use the Magic Wand to select the entire blue background, then choose **Select > Inverse** so you have only the dolphin selected. Copy and paste it into the movie frame. The dolphin will appear as a separate layer, which makes it easy to move around.

Position the dolphin where you'd like it. In my example, shown in Figure 9.9, I've placed her nose at the upper-right corner of the page. Don't worry, the entire dolphin is still there as a separate layer—as long as you don't drop the layer.

Figure 9.9
Blue nose.

Cut That Out!

This technique is referred to by those of us in the "biz" as *cut-out animation*. Traditionally, the animator would use cutouts of photos or illustrations, and then just move them under the camera. Think *Monty Python* or *South Park*.

Moving Right Along

Let's give the dolphin some life. Turn on tracing paper (Cmd/Ctrl+T). Now you can see where the dolphin has been so that you can move her through the water convincingly. To create the next frame, just click the **Step Forward** button. Painter automatically creates a new frame. You can then alternate between moving the dolphin a bit each time and advancing to the next frame to create a simple 40-frame animation.

Since the dolphin is on a separate layer, you can make her smaller with each frame so that she fades into the distance, or you can rotate her so she swims in a circle. For now, we'll just focus on having her move across the screen. When you have reached the 40th frame of your stack, drop the layer and turn the tracing paper off. Click the **Play** button to see your movie. Use Save As to preserve this version in your choice of formats before you continue to develop it.

Bubbling Over

Let's make our animation a bit more interesting by adding some water bubbles. Use the **Splatter Water** brush from the **Watercolor** category and a medium blue to spray some bubbles on each frame. The top of Figure 9.10 shows a default Splatter Water stroke. I eliminated the splattery effect to make the elements look more like bubbles by turning the **Wetness** amount in the **Water** control panel of the Brush Controls down to zero. Figure 9.11 shows my settings.

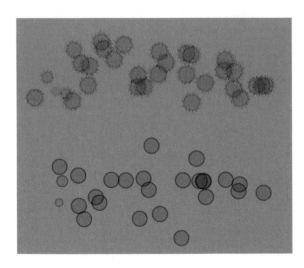

Figure 9.10
Splats and bubbles.

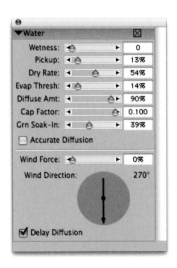

Figure 9.11
Wetness protection.

Watercolor variants create their own layer, which means that if you want to erase or add more bubbles, or edit them in any way, you can do so without disrupting the layer underneath, where the dolphin lives. Using tracing paper, you can also see how much water has been added to the previous layer. To erase on the watercolor layer, use the **Eraser Wet** variant. Be sure to set the color to white.

The realistic white bubbles were made in a completely different way. I added them to some frames by using a large chalk variant with a custom paper texture made from a photo of soda pop foam. They show up nicely in Figure 9.12. Rhoda showed how to capture paper from a photo in Lesson 3, and I'll be making more custom textures in an illustration project in Lesson 10.

Figure 9.12
Refreshing and foamy.

Safe Stax

We hate to nag (although it does run in our families), but please remember to save each version of your animation with a unique name every time you add another effect to the frame stack. Painter can behave in unexpected ways, and it's better to be safe than sorry. So if you're going out, take a sweater.

I added a few swirly lines in white and yellow to create more motion, using the **Smooth Ink Pen** with the opacity set to 50%. Finally, I finished up with the **Wet Oily Blender** variant in **Artists' Oils** to blend some of my splatters and lines. Figure 9.13 shows a frame where dolphins are blending nicely into the peace sign.

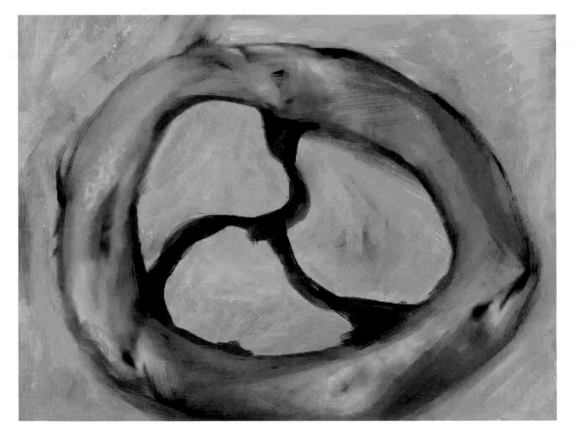

Figure 9.13
Blending in.

Movie Scripts

This has nothing to do with adding dialogue—Painter has no sound capability at all. I'm referring to Painter's system for recording a sequence of brush strokes and/or effects for playback on a blank or existing image. When you click the red **Record** button on the **Scripts** palette, shown in Figure 9.14, everything you do is recorded until you click the **Stop** button. Give the script a name, and it will be added to your Scripts library. To play a script, use the **Playback Script** command in the **Scripts** menu. To apply a script automatically to an entire frame stack, you need the **Apply Script to Movie** command in the **Movie** menu.

Figure 9.14
We are recording.

Keeping Records

Record and play back the script for an entire painting to have a review of your creative process, as all your undos and changes are part of the action. This makes a great demonstration or teaching aid. Brush strokes appearing quickly one after another makes an interesting kind of animation, too.

Royalty-Free Characters

My favorite sources for "artsy" animation are the stopped motion photography of E. Muybridge, who—in the 1870s before the advent of motion pictures—devised a way to create a series of still photographs of animals and people in action. Figure 9.15 shows a sample of Muybridge's remarkable work. Several sets of his photos are available to you in the Lesson 9 folder on the CD. They just need to be opened as numbered files. No worries about copyright infringement after 130 years!

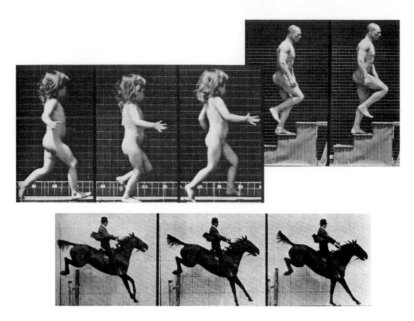

Figure 9.15

Muybridge action photos.

Let's create a script for adding color to a Muybridge frame stack. (There was no color film in 1870!) Open the **MuyDancer source** movie by double-clicking the frame stack or opening the numbered files. A great way to add exciting colors to a grayscale image instantly (my favorite speed) is to apply the colors from a gradient preset. Look at the choices in the Gradients library and find one you like. I picked **Vivid Mixture**. Engage the Record function (red button) on the Scripts palette. Now use the **Express in Image** command from the Gradients popup menu on any frame in the stack. This brings up a **Bias** slider and a preview so you can determine how you want the gradient colors mapped to the luminosity (values) of the image. (Sound familiar? We used this method to prepare Audrey's photo for a portrait painting in Lesson 5.) Figure 9.16 shows the slider position that makes a pleasing color map in my opinion. If you like the result, stop recording and give the script a name. I called mine **Xpress Grad.** If you don't like the result, stop recording and click Cancel. Try again with a different gradient or Bias setting. It's a good idea to undo the action(s) on the frame to return it to the original state before you continue working.

Figure 9.16
Vivid color mapping.

Choose **Apply Script to Movie** and select your new script for playback. Sit back and watch each frame get the color treatment. For
long movies and complex scripts, you can take a leisurely lunch or
coffee break. Play your new version of the movie. Be sure to save it
in QuickTime or AVI format before you continue working.

Smudge-o-Matic

Try making a script with multiple brush strokes. Smudging and
smearing can be used to get painterly effects, especially with bristly
variants like **Smeary Varnish** from the **Impasto** category. But if you
make a script using smeary strokes on the figure in one frame,
those same strokes won't match the figure on other frames. You just
might have to smear the dancer by hand in each frame. But there is
a way to automate smearing of the background in each frame.

Consider recording all the brush strokes needed to make a complete smeary painting on a frame that you have saved as an image, without special attention to the particular pose of the dancer. Save it as a script. Now, instead of using Apply Script to Movie, we'll use the **Playback Script** function on each frame individually. Prepare each frame by making a rough Lasso selection around the figure and inversing the selection so that only the background will be affected by the script. Figure 9.17 shows the end result of smearing all over the image with a **Pointed Stump** from the **Blender** variants.

The woman in Figure 9.18 is surrounded by a loose Lasso selection. Don't spend much time trying to be accurate—the whole idea here is to save time. At this point you'll either choose **Select > Invert** or use the **Draw Outside** option at the lower left of your image window. Use the **Playback** command on the **Scripts** palette and choose your smeary script. Figure 9.19 shows a different frame after the smeary background has been done.

Figure 9.17

Fits into the abstract lesson, too.

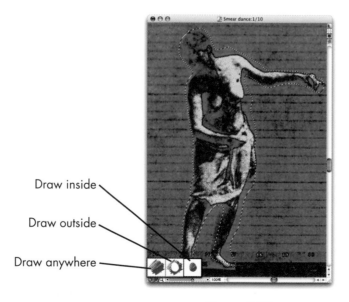

Draw inside

Draw outside

Draw anywhere

Figure 9.18

Get these marching ants off me!

Figure 9.19
Smeared background.

Don't Be Undone

Be very careful that you have the background and not the dancer targeted for script playback. If you make a mistake, there's no going back, even though you haven't stepped forward to the next frame. That's because Undo won't recognize the script command as a single action, but considers each and every brushstroke in the script as a separate item. Even 32 undos (the maximum) might not make much of a dent in this kind of script.

The next stage involves smudging each figure by hand, using painterly strokes with your favorite smeary tools. Figure 9.20 was done mostly with Smeary Varnish and a few Pointed Stump strokes. The style is reminiscent of Paul Gauguin (van Gogh's buddy). This lady was just the right age to be Gauguin's girlfriend!

Figure 9.20
Post-impressionist flavor.

Rotoscope Cloning

Traditional *rotoscoping* is a way to project a single frame from live action footage in perfect alignment with the animator's drawing surface. The animator draws each cel based on the action of the figure in the projected frame, then steps forward to the next frame in the action to draw on the next cel. The classic example is Disney's dancing hippos in the 1940's film *Fantasia*. A real ballerina was filmed dancing, and the footage was projected one frame at time so that the cartoon hippo's actions could be more realistic. It's all about the action, not necessarily re-creating the original figure.

Corel Painter can function as a digital rotoscope! It's just a matter of finding suitable movie (or video) sources or sequences of still images that create action when they are viewed quickly enough. The Muybridge action photos are a great resource, once again. The Lesson 9 folder includes horses jumping, a kid running, and a guy climbing stairs.

Keep Dancing

The basis for rotoscoping in Painter is establishing a frame-by-frame connection between a source frame stack and a destination frame stack. Both stacks must have the same dimensions and number of frames. Let's continue working with the dancer. Use either your color version or the original grayscale sequence. You'll be designating this stack as the clone source and using the tracing paper feature to guide your work on the blank frames.

We need the pixel dimensions of those dancer frames in order to make a new frame stack at the same size. Here's a way to get that info. With any frame active (they're all the same size), choose **Select > All** followed by **Edit > Copy**, then **Edit > Paste into New Image**. Now you can use Canvas > Resize to find out the height and width of the new image. The Resize dialog for the image shown in Figure 9.21 indicates that width is 620 pixels and height is 900 pixels. Select **File > New** and enter the dimensions you have for your new frame stack. Be sure to click the Movie button and enter the number of frames needed. In this case, it's 10. Before you click OK, choose a paper color for the background. I picked a mauve-pink.

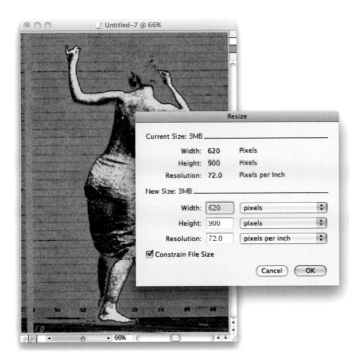

Figure 9.21
Check my size.

Click on the source movie again to make it active and choose **Set Movie Clone Source** from the **Movie** menu, shown in Figure 9.22. Now make the blank stack active and turn on tracing paper. You should see the ghost image of source frame 1 on your blank frame 1. Figure 9.23 shows both the source frame stack and the blank stack. The Frame Stacks palette indicates that frame 1 is active. The title bar on both stacks tells us we are looking at the first of 10 frames.

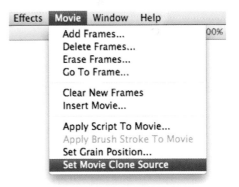

Figure 9.22
Movie menu.

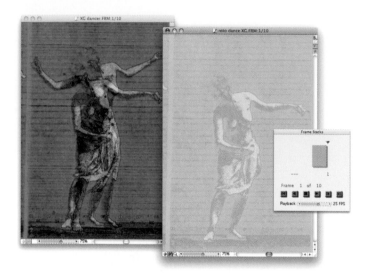

Figure 9.23
May I have this dance?

When you step forward, the ghost image will change to the corresponding frame in the source. Use any brush variant or style you like. Possibilities include the following:

- Accurate outline of the figure with a fine point pen or pencil.

- Sketchy gesture with a larger variant such as conte sticks or oil pastels.

- Painting with one or more cloner variants (or any brush using Clone Color).

- Filling the shape of the figure with scribbles using the Nervous Pen or other quirky variants.

To get more ideas, play the frame stacks of Muybridge rotoscopes I've created over the years using different versions of Painter. Feel free to use a combination of techniques. Consider using different brushes and styles from one frame to the next—a great method for those of us who have a hard time making decisions. I encourage you, as always, to experiment.

Dancing Backward

Let's start rotoscoping this lady. When you finish frame 1 and step forward to frame 2 with tracing paper on, you are seeing not only the source frame, but also the drawing you just made on frame 1. Seeing your work on the previous frame or two is essential if you're creating from scratch, but now it's just getting in the way. What to do? The solution is so simple you've probably thought of it already.

Yes, work backward! If you start on frame 10, there's nothing in frame 9 to intrude. So keep going back a frame at a time and stop when you get to the beginning! Figure 9.24 has some frames from the rotoscoped dancer showing a different Cloner variant in each frame. You can play it (and change it); just open the frame stack file **MuyDancer XG cloned.** (The XG stands for Xpress Gradient.) I suggest roducing the playback rate to about 8 fps.

Figure 9.24
Let's do "The Clone!"

Dance Marathon

Our little 10-frame movie can become more substantial by splicing a number of versions together or adding frame stacks with different actions. The **Insert Movie** command in the **Movie** menu (refer to Figure 9.22) offers a way to combine movies having the same frame dimensions. The number of frames doesn't matter. Convert numbered image files or QuickTime or AVI movies to frame stacks again so they can be accessed with the Insert Movie feature.

What's Next?

Once again, I've kept my promise to you—I haven't covered everything about this subject! But you don't need much hand-holding at this point, and I expect you will continue working on your own. If you like scripted effects, you can use the technique with video footage. If rotoscoping turns you on, be advised that hundreds of Muybridge photo sequences are available on CD. (See the "Resources" section in the Appendix.) Of course, you can rotoscope other images or movies.

Well, if there's anything important I haven't told you about Painter so far, I better do it in the next lesson.

10 Illustration Projects

What's the difference between fine art and illustration? Fine art hangs on the wall, and illustrations get published. Well, that's the idea, but there's a lot of overlap. If you digitize the Mona Lisa and put a pair of jeans on her, you've got an ad. (It's actually been done. Mona's been public domain for even longer than Muybridge photos.) On the other hand, commercial art can hang in a museum after only a few decades. Examples include early 20th-century orange crate labels and the psychedelic posters for 1960s rock concerts.

Unlike a fine art piece, it's easier to know when you're finished with an illustration assignment—the client tells you. Many of the images you've already created with Painter could be used as illustrations under the right circumstances. In this lesson, you'll work on creating images specifically for publication. These assignments will encourage you to combine a variety of techniques covered in early lessons. But first, let's set some type.

Working with Type

In the world of professional print publishing, a graphic designer will typically use a vector-based program like Illustrator or a page-layout program such as InDesign to create the text needed to accompany your illustration. (It's good to own stock in Adobe Systems.) But if a special effect is desired for a few words or letters, it might be necessary to use a pixel-based program and make it part of your image. Both Painter and Photoshop have terrific, but very different, options for text effects.

P.S, I Love You

Text made with page-layout or word processor applications uses Adobe's PostScript technology, allowing crisp high-quality printing at any size (like a vector-based image). Pixel-based programs can only provide bitmap text, which will not look good at small sizes and might even be illegible.

Typography 101

Your Wacom tablet won't be necessary for most of this section, but don't forget where you put it. Even if you know the meaning of *kerning* and can pronounce *leading* correctly, don't skip this part.

Painter's **Text** tool icon is a capital letter T. When it is active, the Property Bar gives you many of the standard choices for font, point size, and alignment. In addition to those settings, you can choose to have a drop shadow or an interior shadow applied automatically as you enter text on your canvas. There are separate color and opacity controls as well as composite method choices for the text and its shadow. Just highlight **Text Attributes** or **Shadow Attributes** to alter them independently. Figure 10.1 gets you acquainted with these options. When you click on your canvas with the Text tool, a special layer is automatically created, with the T symbol showing that this is editable type (see Figure 10.2). Begin typing, and the Layers palette will update to indicate the content.

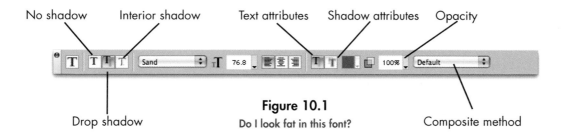

Figure 10.1

Do I look fat in this font?

No shadow Interior shadow Text attributes Shadow attributes Opacity

Drop shadow Composite method

The **Text** palette, shown in Figure 10.3, gives you most of the Property Bar choices and more. Here's where you'll adjust *tracking* (spacing between groups of letters and blocks of text) and *leading* (the spacing between lines of text), and assign a curve style. Blur effects at the bottom of the palette can be assigned to the text or shadow independently.

Figure 10.2

Editable, but not edible.

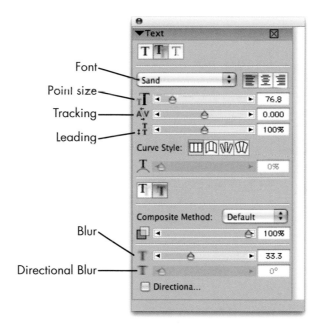

Font

Point size

Tracking

Leading

Blur

Directional Blur

Figure 10.3

Leading rhymes with bedding.

The top left example in Figure 10.4 shows my text in blue with a magenta drop shadow. Other variations were made just by playing with shadows, blurs, and composite methods. The bottom-left text uses the **Reverse-Out** method. The top-right example shows blurred text and no shadow. The bottom right shows the **Screen** method and a 33.3 blur applied only to the shadow.

Figure 10.4

Texting, 1, 2, 3. . .

Kernel of Truth

Painter's Text feature does not provide a way to fine-tune spacing between letter pairs. That's called *kerning*. (Don't let the fact that Painter's tracking icon looks exactly like Photoshop's kerning icon confuse you.) When you're finished editing text, use the **Convert to Default Layer** command in the **Layers** palette popup menu. Then you'll have to kern "by hand"—use the Lasso tool to select a letter to be moved. I did that to the lower-right sample in Figure 10.4.

Rasterize Me!

When you attempt to apply brush strokes or use any commands outside the Text palette, Painter will ask if you want to commit the text to an image (default) layer. If you agree, your text is converted to ordinary pixels. That's called *rasterizing*.

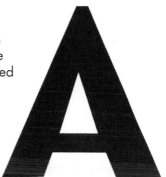

Figure 10.5
A fresh A.

Amazing effects can be applied to letterforms, once they are rasterized. We'll use two dynamic plug-in layers in tandem, **Burn** and **Bevel,** to transform an ordinary letter into an eroded sculptural piece, evoking an ancient mysterious realm. Game designers might see some possibilities here. Figure 10.5 shows a freshly typed and rasterized letter in a font called **Gadget.** I chose a rather hefty sans serif typeface, knowing that some destruction would still leave enough of it intact. Follow along using a similar typeface, such as Arial Black, Charcoal, or Futura.

Choose **Burn** from the **dynamic plug-ins** at the bottom of your **Layers** palette. The settings I used are shown in Figure 10.6 to get the effect in Figure 10.7.

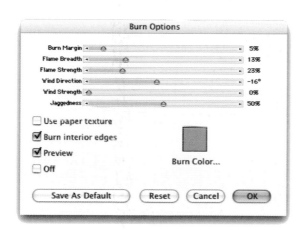

Figure 10.6
Burn, baby, burn!

Figure 10.7
Jagged and ragged.

I Shot the Serif

Sans serif type refers to letterforms that do not have those little "feet" and doodads at the end of a stroke. Those extra bits that finish off the main strokes of a letter are *serifs*.

Me and My Shadow

The external shadow available for text behaves differently from the drop shadow you can add to an image layer. A drop shadow exists on its own layer and can be manipulated separately, independent of its more solid counterpart.

Refer to the settings in Figure 10.8 for the bevel effect shown in Figure 10.9. I also added a drop shadow.

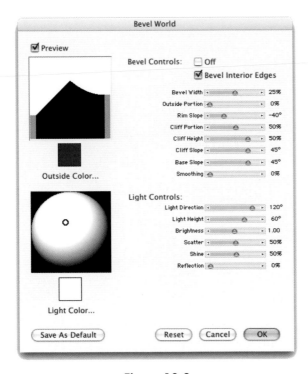

Figure 10.8

Bevel, baby, bevel!

Figure 10.9

Rough and rugged.

When a text layer is rasterized, you can paint it, fill it with a gradient, pattern, or texture, push it, pull it, and stomp on it. Some of those options will be inflicted upon the letter B for a change. Figure 10.10 shows the before version, and Figure 10.11 demonstrates what can happen when good people use too many effects.

Figure 10.10

Innocent B-standers.

Figure 10.11

F-X frenzy.

I certainly don't want to encourage you to torture type, but I do want to explain the cool techniques used here. The shower door effect on the purple B is the result of applying **Effects > Focus > Glass Distortion**. I chose to use **Basic Paper** as the source of luminosity variation. The B in the center shows the result of using **Effects > Surface Control > Distress** with the settings shown in Figure 10.12. Using Grain refers to paper texture. My choice here is Coarse Cotton Canvas.

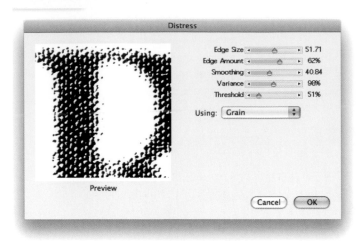

Figure 10.12

B distressed—B very distressed.

Now we come to the melting, disintegrating mess. First, I selected the green letter with the Magic Wand to prevent effects from spilling over the edges (that comes later), then filled it with **Blobs** from the **Esoterica** group in the **Effects** menu. I accepted the default settings for Blobs, shown in Figure 10.13, choosing to fill the blobs with Current Color, which was a bright magenta.

I chose **Edit > Fade** at about 50% to bring back some of the original color. Then I repeated the fill with deep purple and faded it again. There is a lovely randomness about blobs, and you can never get the same effect twice. Figure 10.14 shows these two stages, followed by **Apply Marbling**, also in the Esoterica group of effects.

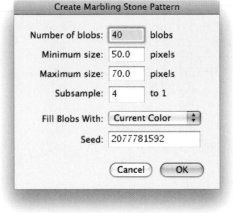

Figure 10.13

Prepare to blob.

Figure 10.14

B is for blobs.

Blobs and Stones

When you apply blobs, the dialog box that comes up is called Create Marbling Stone Pattern. This is because a pattern of blobs is the first stage in creating marbling effects on paper. Marble is a kind of stone, after all.

The real fun begins when you use a dynamic plug-in called **Liquid Lens.** You'll need your Wacom tablet for this part. The Liquid Lens controls shown in Figure 10.15 remain open while you work. There are several items for distorting an image in a fluid way. I like the Brush tool for dragging pixels around. That's how the drippy icicle shapes were made. There's no Undo available, but that Eraser icon represents a tool for restoring or reverting pixels to their original condition. Partial restoration can produce some intriguing effects. As with all dynamic layers, changes can be made later, and (very important) no harm is being done to the layer beneath. Turn off the visibility of the Liquid Lens layer, as shown in Figure 10.16, to see the pristine pre-warp image.

I prefer using this kind of distortion on faces rather than defenseless members of the alphabet. Try it on images in the **People > Heads** folder, or members of your family, or high-ranking government officials.

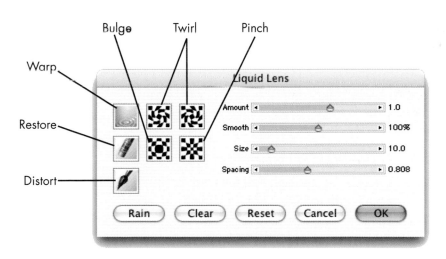

Figure 10.15

The Rain button makes acid rain.

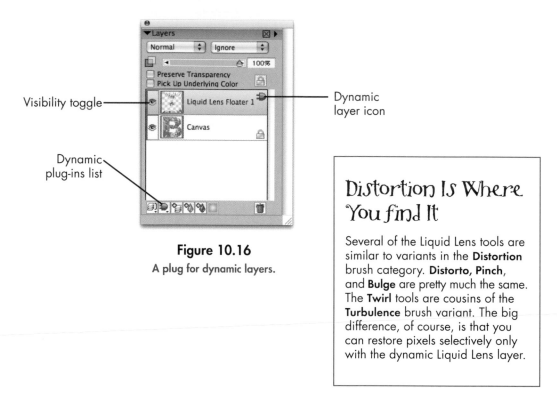

Visibility toggle

Dynamic layer icon

Dynamic plug-ins list

Figure 10.16
A plug for dynamic layers.

Distortion Is Where You Find It

Several of the Liquid Lens tools are similar to variants in the **Distortion** brush category. **Distorto, Pinch**, and **Bulge** are pretty much the same. The **Twirl** tools are cousins of the **Turbulence** brush variant. The big difference, of course, is that you can restore pixels selectively only with the dynamic Liquid Lens layer.

Design a Poster

Work along with me on an assignment to create the text and graphics for an event called "Open Mike." The source photos of vintage microphones shown in Figure 10.17 are part of a collection provided in the Lesson 10 folder on the CD that accompanies this book.

Layouts

It's customary for an illustrator or designer to make quick *thumbnail* (small) sketches or layouts as the first step. Well, maybe the second step after a discussion about what the client wants. Digital sketches can include quick surface or tonal effects and layered images combined with different composite methods. This part of the process can be fun because your creativity is free to roam. Follow a theme or branch off in another direction, or both. It's easy to make multiple variations on an image digitally. Just remember to use **Iterative Save** so the flow of ideas won't be interrupted. And don't overwhelm your client by displaying all the possibilities—just two or three of your best efforts.

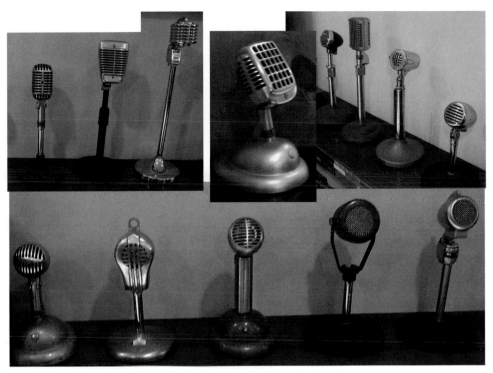

Figure 10.17
Step up to the mike.

Figure 10.18 shows three of the mike photos layered on a black background using the following composite methods, from left to right: Difference, Luminosity, Screen. I liked the colors and the geometric shapes resulting from the overlap of rectangles.

Figure 10.18
Layered layout.

Another layout using the same three images is shown in Figure 10.19. This time the background is a golden yellow, and each of the image elements has been posterized (how appropriate). That's a command you'll find in **Effects > Tonal Control**. It reduces the continuous tone of a photo to a smaller number of "levels," or flat color shapes. I also added pixels to the vertical dimension, using Canvas > Canvas Size, to get a standard poster format and to make room for text.

I looked for a font with a perfect circle for the letter O so I could use it in the word "Open." Gill Sans was ideal, and I had it in a family of weights ranging from light to ultra bold. In Painter, all the text in a given block of type must be the same color and point size, so that big yellow O in Figure 10.20 is on its own layer.

Figure 10.19
Posterized poster.

Figure 10.20
No serifs here.

When I tried to tilt the "Open Mike" text, I was prompted to commit the text to an image layer. Painter requires that you rasterize type before you can use Transform commands, such as Rotate. This turned out to be an advantage, allowing me to fill individual letter shapes with different colors using the Paint Bucket.

Riffing

I changed the background color to purple for the composite in Figure 10.21. The composite methods for the mikes have also been changed. The mike on the left uses the **Lighten** method, and its opacity is 60%. The center mike uses the **Screen** method, and the mike on the right uses **Hard Light** at 70% opacity.

The variation in Figure 10.22 is a hip style perfect for Blues night. The background is blue, of course. All three mikes are now in Luminosity mode, which uses the hue of the background but the values (luminosity) of the layer. I sketched playful black lines with the **Leaky Marker** variant and white lines with the **Scratchboard** tool from the **Pens** group.

Figure 10.21
A hard day's light.

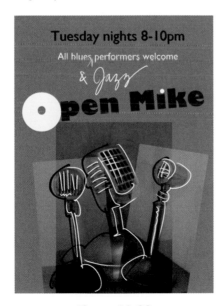

Figure 10.22
Open to blues mode.

Family Style

Barbara Pollak is back once again, this time to provide a step-by-step process for one of the whimsical family portraits she creates. See more examples of her unique style at www.freckleshop.com. Figure 10.23 shows an illustration of her own family in an idyllic Hawaiian setting. Take it from here, Babs.

Figure 10.23
Family luau.

Mahalo, Rhoda! As an illustrator, I am always looking for ways to challenge myself and have fun with my work. In this family portrait, I incorporate the following Painter tools: Cloner brushes, Acrylic brushes, working in layers, and the Image Hose.

Start with a Sketch

Like many illustrators, I need to surround myself with reference images so that I can portray my subjects accurately. It also helps me generate ideas. I have two ginormous filing cabinets filled with photos just of kids' facial expressions!

Once I figure out the background, I put together a sketch and then scan it at high resolution, around 300 dpi. I open a new document with the final size and position my sketch to fill the space. It doesn't matter if the pencil lines are a bit blurred, since I will be painting over them. Figure 10.24 shows my pencil sketch.

Figure 10.24
Sketch and scan.

Color and Texture

I want to get a feel for overall color. Working in layers, I can easily block in background colors. At this point there should be a layer with the sketch on it over a blank canvas. You can use the blank canvas for color, as long as you select **Darken** (or **Gel** or **Multiply**) as the composite method for the sketch layer. This will enable you to see the colors through your sketch. The left half of Figure 10.25 shows color visible through the sketch, and the right half is what the color looks like when visibility of the sketch layer is turned off. Not too pretty, eh?

Figure 10.25
Sketch on and sketch off.

My next move is to add a bit of texture. I'll use a scan of my husband's retro patterned Hawaiian shirt as a Clone Source. You can see it in Figure 10.26, and you'll find **hawaiifabric.jpg** in the source images folder for this lesson on the CD. I open the Hawaiian shirt scan and my layered illustration at the same time. With the **Straight Cloner** variant, I use the **Option/Alt+click** technique to designate the origin point on the shirt image. Then I paint the shirt texture directly onto the color layer of the composite. The same basic technique was used to clone the texture for the table and chairs from photos of wicker furniture.

Figure 10.26
Shirt's up!

After I "Hawaiianized" Steve's shirt, I used the **Diffuse Blur** brush
from the **Photo** category to soften the texture around the edges.
I also gave it a slight purple cast by choosing a grayish purple in the
Colors palette and selecting the shirt, then applying **Effects > Surface
Control > Color Overlay** with the settings shown in Figure 10.27. To
clean up this illustration a bit more, I can use the eraser side of my
Wacom pen to remove the pencil marks on the sketch layer.

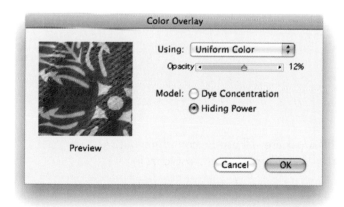

Figure 10.27
Color overlay.

Grass and Flowers

My daughter's grass skirt looks like it might have been cloned from a scan or a photo, but it was actually painted with an Acrylic variant. Practice using the **Acrylic Opaque Detail** brush. You'll need to work on a new layer for this part. Notice that this brush has built-in color variability, about 3% Hue and 11% Value. The organic-looking variations within a stroke are partially due to its being a **Rake** stroke type. I overlapped several strokes using a medium-saturation yellow, then applied a drop shadow. An additional layer with a slightly different yellow and another drop shadow gave me quite a lot of depth and realism. I used the same techniques for the palm fronds. Figure 10.28 shows several sample strokes with and without drop shadows. Choose **Effects > Objects > Create Drop Shadow** and accept the default settings in the dialog box.

Figure 10.28

Acrylic skirt and leaves.

The Shadow Knows

You can change the opacity and position of the drop shadow later because it will automatically exist on its own layer as part of a group. Figure 10.29 shows the group opened with the shadow selected.

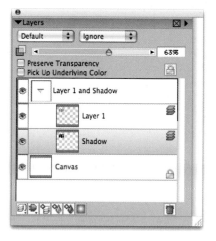

Figure 10.29
Shadows sold separately.

I like the look of mixing painterly Images with photorealistic images. I think this gives my work a warmer and (sometimes) surreal feel. Besides cloning from scans, I occasionally make use of Painter's unique Image Hose to spray items I like onto my illustrations. I have some favorite Painter nozzles, and I even create my own unique nozzles from scans of candy, coins, coffee beans, Polly Pocket dolls, and so on. In this illustration, I sprayed some passionflowers to decorate the waist of my daughter's grass skirt to further incorporate the Hawaiian theme. (See Lesson 7 for a discussion on using the Image Hose.) When I was ready to add this finishing touch, I selected the **Image Hose** from the **Brush Selector Bar** and chose the **Linear-Size-W** variant. The **Passionflower** nozzle can be found in the default **Nozzle** library.

Wheel Bearings

Why choose to have size a function of W (wheel)? I wanted all the flowers to be the same size, so I did not want to have the expression of size be either P (pressure) or R (random). **Linear-Angle-W** or **Linear-Angle-B** (bearing) would also work to prevent size changes.

Figure 10.30 shows how to use the Brush Creator to fiddle around with the Spacing control panel until you're happy with the way flowers line up without too much overlap. The Passionflower nozzle elements, along with a close-up of the finished skirt, are shown in Figure 10.31.

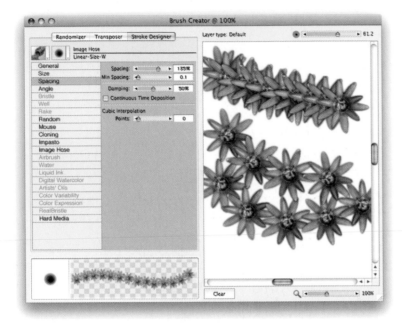

Figure 10.30

Space yourself.

To try out this brush without too much risk, you can create a new layer and then spray onto that layer before committing to the final image.

Figure 10.31

Aloha!

What's Next?

That's all, folks! You've finished your tour of Painter 11. I hope you enjoyed the ride. Your ticket is still good if you want to go again.

Rasa Vitalia

A fundamentals and Beyond

In these few pages, you'll find some useful recommendations for continuing with digital painting after you've finished the book. But first, there are a few things to discuss that will get you off on the right foot.

Pixels vs. Vectors

Programs like Corel Painter and Adobe Photoshop are pixel-based. The word *pixel* is short for **pic**ture **el**ement, using the common abbreviation "pix" for "picture." Each pixel represents a tiny colored dot or square, and with enough of them lined up horizontally and vertically, you'll get the picture. Resolution, measured in pixels per inch or ppi, tells you about the quality of the image. A resolution of 300 ppi has a much finer grain and more detail than the same image at 72 ppi. Resolution is especially important when images are prepared for printing. Pixel-based (also called *raster* or *bitmap*) images must include information on the color and location of every single one of those pixels. Depending on the dimensions and resolution, there can be thousands of such pixels in an image, resulting in hefty file sizes. For example, a Painter or Photoshop file that's 8x10 inches at 300 ppi weighs in at 20MB. The larger the file size, the more RAM is needed and the harder your computer has to work. Older machines can really start huffing and puffing.

By contrast, *vector*-based programs, like Flash and Illustrator, are resolution-independent and have the advantage of smaller files. This is because the images are not composed of stacks of pixels but paths with simple fills and strokes (outlines) that can be stored as mathematical instructions. By their nature, vector-based images tend to have hard-edged lines with no thickness variation and flat color fills, whereas pixel-based graphics can have the kind of variation (called *continuous tone*) seen in photos and paintings. Working with pixels is intuitive and natural, in my opinion, but it takes considerable practice to get skilled at placing the anchor points and adjusting the curves that make up vector shapes.

The eyes in Figure A.1 show you the difference between pixels and vectors rather dramatically. The photo is zoomed in so you can see some pixels up close and personal. Some smears with a **Blender** variant made the painterly version, and it's obvious which eye was made with vector shapes. There are pros and cons to each approach, and you don't have to restrict yourself to just one or the other. If you're not sure which category you prefer, ask yourself if you'd rather have precision or instant gratification. Do you like being able to create clean, sharp lines or juicy, smeary ones? I knew I was a pixel-packin' mama from the start!

Can't We Just Get Along?

Pixel pushers can have access to some of the benefits of the vector world. Both Painter and Photoshop have tools for drawing and manipulating vector shapes. You can even open Adobe Illustrator files that are in AI (Adobe Illustrator) or EPS (Encapsulated PostScript) format and see each shape in your Layers palette. Of course, these vector images must eventually be converted to pixels, or *rasterized*, which sounds much more exotic.

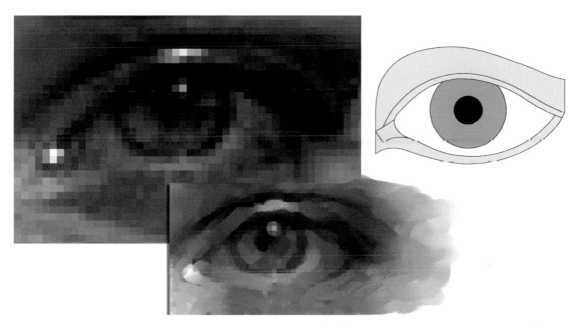

Figure A.1

To smear or not to smear? That is the question!

Nice Save!

I just mentioned two file formats used by vector images: AI and EPS. Here's a list of the most basic file formats used by Painter and other pixel-based applications, along with hints on how to choose the best one for your purposes:

- **RIFF (Raster Image File Format)**: This is Painter's native format, and images you create in Painter are automatically saved as RIFF files. You need this file format to preserve elements unique to Painter, such as Dynamic, Watercolor, or Liquid Ink layers. RIFF files are not recognized by other applications.

- **PSD (Photoshop Document)**: If your Painter image has default layers (not specialized layers, such as Dynamic, Watercolor, or Liquid Ink), and you want to switch easily between Painter and Photoshop, use the PSD format. Painter's masks will be preserved as Photoshop channels. Unfortunately, not all of Painter's composite methods have equivalents to Photoshop blending modes, and text layers will not survive the transition.

- **TIFF (Tagged Image File Format)**: This popular format will not preserve layers, dropping them all into the background. One mask can be saved if you use the Save Alpha check box. (*Alpha* is Photoshop's term for additional channels created from saved selection masks.)

- **JPEG (Joint Photographic Experts Group)**: A very handy format for compressing an image file to make it load quickly on a website or transmit quickly as an email attachment. This compression is *lossy*, meaning the quality of an image will suffer if it is compressed over and over or if low quality settings are used. Be sure to save a copy of your image in another format that will keep its quality intact.

- **GIF (Graphics Interchange Format)**: This is the option specifically designed for most non-photographic images used on the web. Colors are reduced to 256 or fewer, and you have several choices for minimizing file size.

- **PNG (Portable Network Graphics)**: Using a *lossless* compression method, this format is superior to GIF for transferring images on the Internet. For one thing, PNG allows portions of an image to be transparent. Painter 11 is the first version to be PiNG-able.

- **PICT (short for "Picture"):** (Sorry, you were probably expecting a cool acronym, like "Please Insert Clever Tag.") Often chosen for multimedia programs. You can save a Painter movie as a series of numbered PICT files and export them to other animation applications.

Show Us Your Gamuts

Advanced color theory and techniques for optimizing image color are beyond the scope of this book. But a basic color primer will help get you started. Here are the color terms and concepts used in this book and a few more for good measure.

- **HSV (Hue, Saturation, and Value):** Hue is a position on the spectrum. The words *red*, *orange*, and *green* refer to hues but are very inexact. We need to know how pure the color is (saturation) and how bright or dark (value) it is. Other terms for value are *brightness*, *lightness*, and *luminosity*. Figure A.2 shows HSV values displayed as numerical settings in the Colors palette. The popup menu for the Colors palette gives you an option for switching to a display of RGB sliders.

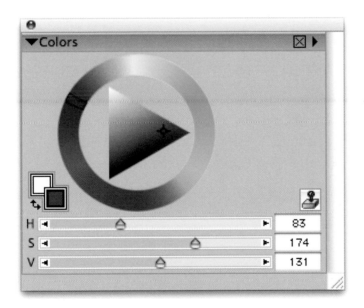

Figure A.2

A specific bright red.

- **RGB:** The red, green, and blue components of a color, also available as numerical settings in the Colors palette. The RGB color model is additive, involving colors emitted from a light source. The RGB color space is useful for describing colors on your monitor.

- **CMYK**: The cyan, magenta, yellow, and black components of a color. We use K for black because B is already taken. This color space is subtractive, involving reflected color from a mixture of paints, dyes, or inks. Painter does not use the CMYK color space, but you can choose between RGB and CMYK when you save a Painter file as a Photoshop document.

- **Gamut:** The entire range of colors that are available in a given color space. RGB has a larger gamut than CMYK, especially for highly saturated colors. This explains why some colors that look great on your monitor don't look so good in print.

Painter provides a color management feature, available in the Canvas menu. The settings include the usual suspects for assigning and converting to color profiles. Your choice of profile depends on your purpose, such as the kind of printing you plan to do, and you might need to ask an expert for advice. Turn color management on and off with its icon in the upper-right edge of your image window. Its neighbors are the toggles for tracing paper, grid, and Impasto (depth). When color management is enabled, the icon is a set of brightly colored bars. When this feature is off, the icon is black. Hover your mouse over the icon to see what color profile is assigned to the current image. Click on the icon to get a menu for making changes to your color settings. The left side of Figure A.3 shows color management is on, and the right side shows the popup menu open. Figure A.4 shows the Color Management Settings dialog box.

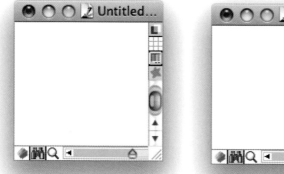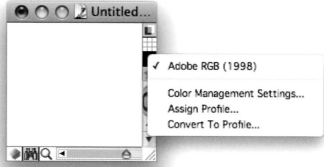

Figure A.3
Show us your profile.

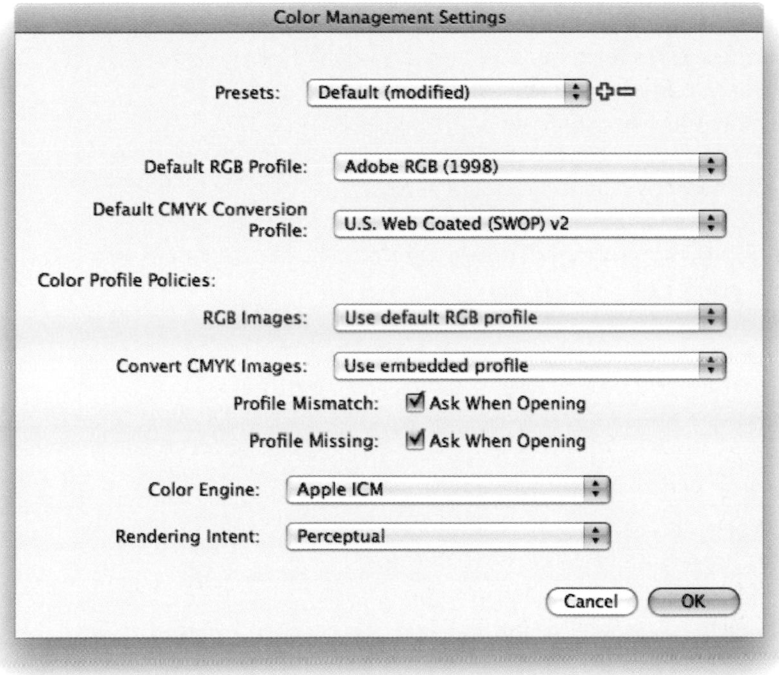

Color Management Settings

Presets: Default (modified)

Default RGB Profile: Adobe RGB (1998)

Default CMYK Conversion Profile: U.S. Web Coated (SWOP) v2

Color Profile Policies:

RGB Images: Use default RGB profile

Convert CMYK Images: Use embedded profile

Profile Mismatch: ☑ Ask When Opening

Profile Missing: ☑ Ask When Opening

Color Engine: Apple ICM

Rendering Intent: Perceptual

Cancel   OK

Figure A.4
Your settings may differ.

Take Two Tablets and
Call Me in the Morning

Actually, only one tablet is needed, no matter how many computers you may have. If you're shopping around for a graphics tablet, I'll make things easier for you. Wacom Technologies is the only manufacturer to consider, and I'm not getting any kickbacks. They make a range of tablets in several sizes for every budget and work situation. Starting with the petite entry-level 4x6-inch BambooFun for about $100 to the Cintiq, which is actually a monitor you can draw on, for about $2000. If you can simply learn to look up at your regular screen while your pen is working down below on your desk or in your lap, you can save $1900! Just look at the cursor to see where to paint. (See, doesn't that prove I'm not on the Wacom payroll?)

It's easy to use a pen tablet because every point on the tablet has a matching point on the screen. When you move your pen over the tablet, the cursor moves in precisely the same way on the screen. Where you touch your pen tip to the tablet is where you click. If you need to establish or customize this "mapping" relationship, use the Wacom Tablet preferences, shown in Figure A.5. This is the Mac version, found in System Preferences. The way to find Wacom preferences on a PC is as follows: Click on Start > All Programs > Wacom Tablet > Wacom Tablet Properties. These are the default settings for mapping. Notice that Pen mode is selected rather than Mouse mode. That's very important to ensure the point-to-point matching of screen and tablet. You'll probably want the full screen mapped to the full tablet area, but there are other options. You can also specify different settings for different applications.

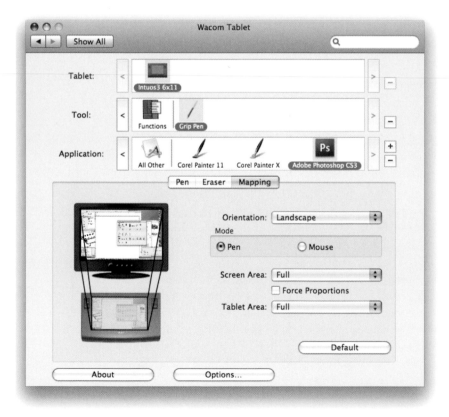

Figure A.5

Tablet mapping.

Figure A.6 shows a portion of the Preferences pane with the settings available for your Wacom pen. Several variables can be adjusted to customize pen behavior, including choices for the Click functions of the lever on the side of some pen barrels.

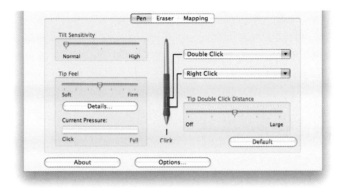

Figure A.6
Click and double-click.

The Graphire tablet shown in Figure A.7 is being used for tracing an image placed under the transparent frame that comes with most tablets. This particular model is Bluetooth capable, so no pesky cord is required. You get a cordless mouse, too.

Figure A.7
Drawing hand sold separately.

My personal choice is the mid-range Intuos series, with more levels of pressure sensitivity than a Graphire or Bamboo tablet. I prefer the very portable 6x8-inch model. There are several sizes, all the way up to 12x18 inches. Wacom tablets come bundled with Painter Essentials, the "lite" version of Corel Painter, as well as Photoshop Elements, the stripped-down version of that other pixel-based program. The Wacom website (www.wacom.com) is as user-friendly as can be, offering you help in deciding which tablet is best for you, downloads for updating drivers (software), technical support, and even a Tips and Tricks section for users of Painter, Photoshop, and Flash.

What's Your Preference?

In Lesson 1, I mentioned **Brush Tracking,** found in **Corel Painter > Preferences.** That's where you can make a test stroke to set the tablet's sensitivity to your touch. Use it any time you feel the need for an adjustment. This is much faster and easier than using the Wacom Tablet preferences.

The **General Preferences** dialog box shown in Figure A.8 has several settings you'll want to customize sooner or later. The sooner the better for **Units**. It's set at pixels by default. I just can't help thinking in inches sometimes, and that's available. Europeans and other civilized folks can choose centimeters. There are points and picas for you typesetters and columns for you neo-classical architects.

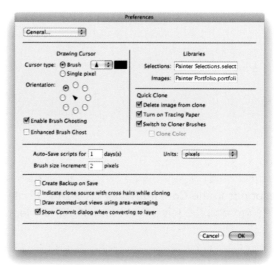

Figure A.8

Cursors and units and more.

With **Brush Ghosting** enabled, the cursor becomes the shape of your current brush tip when your pen hovers over the tablet. **Enhanced Brush Ghosting** (Painter X and 11) shows the angle and direction of your pen while you're working. These options can slow you down if you're using some of the more complex brushes and your computer isn't on steroids. While your brush is moving, what do you want the drawing cursor to look like? There are several choices here, from a tiny triangle to a tiny brush icon, with color options and a choice of orientation to accommodate either your handedness or your lifestyle.

As for **Quick Clone** (introduced in Painter IX), I recommend you accept the defaults, enabling all three options. That's what makes it "quick." And if you're into quickness, you might want to change **Brush Size Increment** to two or three pixels so that when you use the bracket keys to reduce or enlarge your brush size on the fly, changes will be bigger with each click. I disabled the automatic backup feature to avoid cluttering up my hard drive with copies of image files. But I like seeing the Commit warning when I'm about to convert a special layer to a default layer, so I left that checked. Feel free to change other settings when you feel the need.

"Undo" has its own section in the Painter Preferences. The maximum is 32, but it's hard to imagine you'll ever need even half of that. Setting the number of undos to a much lower figure will reduce the drain on your computer's memory.

Different Strokes

Another excellent way to increase speed and efficiency (if you're into that sort of thing) is to learn the keyboard shortcuts for the most frequently used commands, as shown in Table A.1. Some of these are specific to Painter, but most are used by other programs, so you might know them already. A couple of modifier keys are different for Mac and PC users. On the Windows platform, the **Ctrl** key corresponds to the **Command** key on a Mac (that's the key with the Apple logo and the thing that looks like a four-leaf clover with an eating disorder). The **Alt** key on a PC is equivalent to the **Option** key for Mac users. There are a few other differences, like **Delete on a PC** serving the same purpose as the Mac's **Backspace** key.

Table A.1 Keyboard Shortcuts

Menu Command	Mac	PC
File > New	Cmd+N	Ctrl+N
File > Open	Cmd+O	Ctrl+O
File > Save	Cmd+S	Ctrl+S
File > Save As	Shift+Cmd+S	Shift+Ctrl+S
File > Iterative Save	Option+Cmd+S	Alt+Ctrl+S
File > Close	Cmd+W	Ctrl+W
File > Print	Cmd+P	Ctrl+P
Edit > Undo	Cmd+Z	Ctrl+Z
Edit > Copy	Cmd+C	Ctrl+C
Edit > Paste	Cmd+V	Ctrl+V
Select > All	Cmd+A	Ctrl+A
Select > None (Deselect)	Cmd+D	Ctrl+D
Select > Hide/Show Marquee	Shift+Cmd+H	Shift+Ctrl+H
Window > Zoom In	Cmd+ (plus sign)	Ctrl+ (plus sign)
Window > Zoom Out	Cmd+ (minus sign)	Ctrl+ (minus sign)
Window > Zoom to Fit	Cmd+0 (zero)	Ctrl+0 (zero)
Window > Screen Mode Toggle	Cmd+M	Ctrl+M

Get Off My Intellectual Property!

Here's some free legal advice, and I assure you it's worth every penny. If you scan images printed in books or magazines or search the web for digital pictures, be aware that such items might be copyright protected. That's not a problem unless you want to publish your edited versions. Copyright law gives the original creator of an image all rights to it, including derivations thereof. (Or is it "wherefrom"?) How much would you have to change an image to make it legally your own and not just a derivation? Are you willing to go to court to find out?

When it comes to using the likeness of a celebrity, things can get complicated. Are you infringing on the copyright of the subject or the photographer who created the photo? Maybe both. Famous people have the *right of publicity* to prevent others from making money with their likeness, even after death. On the other hand, ordinary folks have the right to privacy, so you need to get a *model release* signed before you can legally publish their faces.

There are exceptions to copyright protection, called *fair use*. For example, you can publish doctored images of famous people for satirical purposes. A copyright expires 70 years after the death of the creator (last time I checked), after which the image becomes *public domain*—so anything goes. An image like the Mona Lisa is *way* in the public domain, even though the actual painting is owned by the Louvre in Paris. Ownership of a piece of art is completely separate from usage rights thereto. The images made available to you on the CD that comes with this book are provided only for your personal use in working the projects. All other rights are reserved by the copyright holders.

Resources

This section suggests sources for more training, images to play with, media to print on, and even places to display your work to other digital painters.

If you have an Internet connection, you have instant access to online tutorials and the Painter community. When you launch Painter 11, you'll see a dialog similar to Figure A.9 with several handy options on the left and samples of Painter artwork on the right. These whimsical creatures are by a Japanese artist. Many other samples by Painter masters are available at the click of a mouse.

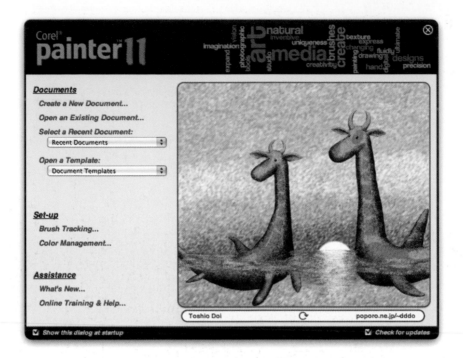

Figure A.9
Whacky giraffes and more.

Click Online Training & Help, and you'll be taken to the Painter 11 page on the Corel website. The Related Information section on the right side of that page has links to the following:

- Tutorials

- Tips & Tricks

- Painter Canvas Newsletter: A "forum for Painter aficionados to learn new tips and techniques, to share and download custom brushes and product freebies, and to discuss all things Painter."

- Painterfactory.com Community: Blogs and discussion of Painter issues and galleries of high-end Painter art.

- Corel Painter Magazine

If you're using Painter IX or X, don't be too quick to dismiss the Welcome screen, shown in Figure A.10. Use the tabs along the edges of the "open book" format to get help and encouragement, as well as a peek at the work of other Painter artists. The **Extra Content** tab, shown here, has a link to online tips and tricks that give you more insight into features and techniques that I might have left out or glossed over. The bottom tab, **Painter on the Net**, sends you to a series of **Quick Tips** that simply tell you what a feature does and how to access it.

Figure A.10
You're welcome.

Finding Images

If you enjoyed working with the stop-motion photos by Muybridge in Lesson 9, you might want to buy the entire collection from Dover Publications. There are two slim volumes, *Muybridge's Animals in Motion* and *Muybridges's Human Figure in Motion*, that provide not only a printed catalog showing each photo sequence, but all images on a CD as electronic clip art. For only $14.95 ($22.50 Canadian), you get enough raw material to keep rotoscoping for years. Are these images royally-free and in the public domain? You betcha— Muybridge died in 1904.

You'll probably want to shoot most of your own source photos, but when you need a variety of images or something unusual in a hurry, use the Internet. If you don't mind low resolution and are careful about possible copyright issues, use Google's search engine. When you get to the Google home page (www.google.com), click on Images instead of Web, and type in what you're looking for. This is a great way to get visual references for accuracy or just browse for ideas.

Way Beyond Disney

I mentioned the dancing hippos from Disney's 1940 film *Fantasia* when I introduced rotoscope animation. There are more recent and much more exciting examples. The Beatles' *Yellow Submarine* (1968) used the rotoscope technique in the "Lucy in the Sky with Diamonds" sequence. Brilliant colors and brush work change every few frames for a gorgeous, splashy effect that's breathtaking even if you're not taking a psychedelic substance. A much darker, gothic style is used in the rotoscoped portions of Ralph Bakshi's highly original *Wizards* (1977). Finally, Richard Linklater's sci-fi thriller, *A Scanner Darkly* (2006), is a rotoscope tour de force—every frame was drawn and painted from live action footage, yielding effects that would be impossible any other way.

There are commercial online sources for high-quality stock photography. They generally require payment of fees for specified usage, and their target market is professional designers and illustrators. If you want a lot of images, those fees can really add up. For stock images with a liberal licensing agreement at bargain prices, my vote goes to ShutterStock.com. It's easy to use their Boolean search engine to find what you need quickly, and best of all, you can subscribe for a relatively small fee, considering the volume of images you'll get. One month of this service costs $249 last time I checked, and it allows you 25 images per day or a total of 750 photos for the month. That's about 33 cents per image. Check it out at www.shutterstock.com.

Consider using your older (analog) photos. Take old snapshots out of the family album or the shoebox and digitize them. A basic scanner is pretty cheap, and it is a handy device to have around. If you want to digitize images found in books or magazines, your scanner should have a Descreen feature. This is needed to prevent an unsightly *moiré pattern* from the halftone dots used in process printing. Published images are almost certainly copyright protected; this is not a problem if you're just using them in the privacy of your own home and with consenting adults.

Color Printing

I've got an inexpensive Canon inkjet printer that I use for most of my letter-size printing. I can get spectacular results as long as I use high-quality paper or other media. Ordinary paper is too porous, letting ink spread into the fibers, so images get blurry or muddy looking. Remember that the colors on your screen have a wider *gamut* (range) than you can achieve with ink on paper. Given the gamut limitations that come with the territory, my choice for crisp rich color is glossy photo paper. Epson and HP make it, among others. It comes in various weights and can be glossy on both sides.

For wearable art, consider printing your images on iron-on transfers that can be applied to clothing, hats, or what-have-you. Avery makes inkjet magnet sheets, which I print with several small images (like the gesture drawings I showed you in Lesson 8). Then I trim them into shapes for some unique refrigerator magnets.

Archival-quality media are available for fine art printing from your desktop. A great resource is www.inkjetart.com, where you can find letter-size or larger canvas (glossy or matte), watercolor paper, and printable fabrics. If you know you'll print on canvas, you won't need to add an optical canvas texture to the artwork.

If you want to print BIG but don't want to invest In a large format printer, order from an outfit like Imagers: www.imagers.com/poster.html. They can print posters and banners on photo paper, film, vinyl, or canvas. Another company, youHuge.com, offers poster-size prints that can be mounted on foam core or other boards. Check them out at http://_youhuge.com/large_format_posters.htm.

Fonts

After using the Text tool for a while, you might get a hankering for more exciting typefaces than just the ones factory-installed on your computer. Lots of fonts are available free for personal (non-commercial) use. They can be downloaded from sites like Larabie Fonts (www.larabiefonts.com) or Blue Vinyl fonts (www.bvfonts.com). Use your favorite search engine to find more font resources on the web. When I entered "free fonts" in a Google search, www.1001freefonts.com was near the top of the list. There are actually 10,000 fonts you can browse alphabetically and download for either Windows or Mac. For the nominal fee of $19.95, you can download all 10,000 fonts at once with a single click. Okay, not quite free, but that's a sweet deal!

If you need a special font and are willing to pay a little more for it, there are quite a few possibilities. LetterHead Fonts specializes in rare and unique fonts for artists and designers and has an elegant website:www.letterheadfonts.com.

The P22 Foundry (www.p22.com) proudly announces that it "creates computer typefaces inspired by Art, History, and sometimes Science. . . ." Pretty impressive, and P22 fonts are available for about $30. Incidentally, many type houses still call themselves *foundries*, even though they hardly ever need to pour molten metal into molds anymore.

Fonthead Design (http://fonthead.com) sells distinctive display fonts in sets of about a dozen for $29 to $59 per volume. Pretty good for such delights as LogJam, Butterfinger, Ladybug, Cyber Monkey, and Bonkers. Fonthead also offers a few freebies, including some whimsical fonts, like Good Dog and SpillMilk, and a set of cartoon face dingbats (small decorative images or symbols) called Font Heads.

Index

License Agreement/Notice of Limited Warranty

By opening the sealed disc container in this book, you agree to the following terms and conditions. If, upon reading the following license agreement and notice of limited warranty, you cannot agree to the terms and conditions set forth, return the unused book with unopened disc to the place where you purchased it for a refund.

License:

The enclosed software is copyrighted by the copyright holder(s) indicated on the software disc. You are licensed to copy the software onto a single computer for use by a single user and to a backup disc. You may not reproduce, make copies, or distribute copies or rent or lease the software in whole or in part, except with written permission of the copyright holder(s). You may transfer the enclosed disc only together with this license, and only if you destroy all other copies of the software and the transferee agrees to the terms of the license. You may not decompile, reverse assemble, or reverse engineer the software.

Notice of Limited Warranty:

The enclosed disc is warranted by Course Technology to be free of physical defects in materials and workmanship for a period of sixty (60) days from end user's purchase of the book/disc combination. During the sixty-day term of the limited warranty, Course Technology will provide a replacement disc upon the return of a defective disc.

Limited Liability:

THE SOLE REMEDY FOR BREACH OF THIS LIMITED WARRANTY SHALL CONSIST ENTIRELY OF REPLACE-MENT OF THE DEFECTIVE DISC. IN NO EVENT SHALL COURSE TECHNOLOGY OR THE AUTHOR BE LIABLE FOR ANY OTHER DAMAGES, INCLUDING LOSS OR CORRUPTION OF DATA, CHANGES IN THE FUNCTIONAL CHARACTERISTICS OF THE HARDWARE OR OPERATING SYSTEM, DELETERIOUS INTERACTION WITH OTHER SOFTWARE, OR ANY OTHER SPECIAL, INCIDENTAL, OR CONSEQUENTIAL DAMAGES THAT MAY ARISE, EVEN IF COURSE TECHNOLOGY AND/OR THE AUTHOR HAS PREVIOUSLY BEEN NOTIFIED THAT THE POSSIBILITY OF SUCH DAMAGES EXISTS.

Disclaimer of Warranties:

COURSE TECHNOLOGY AND THE AUTHOR SPECIFICALLY DISCLAIM ANY AND ALL OTHER WARRANTIES, EITHER EXPRESS OR IMPLIED, INCLUDING WARRANTIES OF MERCHANTABILITY, SUITABILITY TO A PARTICULAR TASK OR PURPOSE, OR FREEDOM FROM ERRORS. SOME STATES DO NOT ALLOW FOR EXCLUSION OF IMPLIED WARRANTIES OR LIMITATION OF INCIDENTAL OR CONSEQUENTIAL DAMAGES, SO THESE LIMITATIONS MIGHT NOT APPLY TO YOU.

Other:

This Agreement is governed by the laws of the State of Massachusetts without regard to choice of law principles. The United Convention of Contracts for the International Sale of Goods is specifically disclaimed. This Agreement constitutes the entire agreement between you and Course Technology regarding use of the software.